The International Design Library®

Italian Renaissance Textile Designs

by Dolores M. Andrew

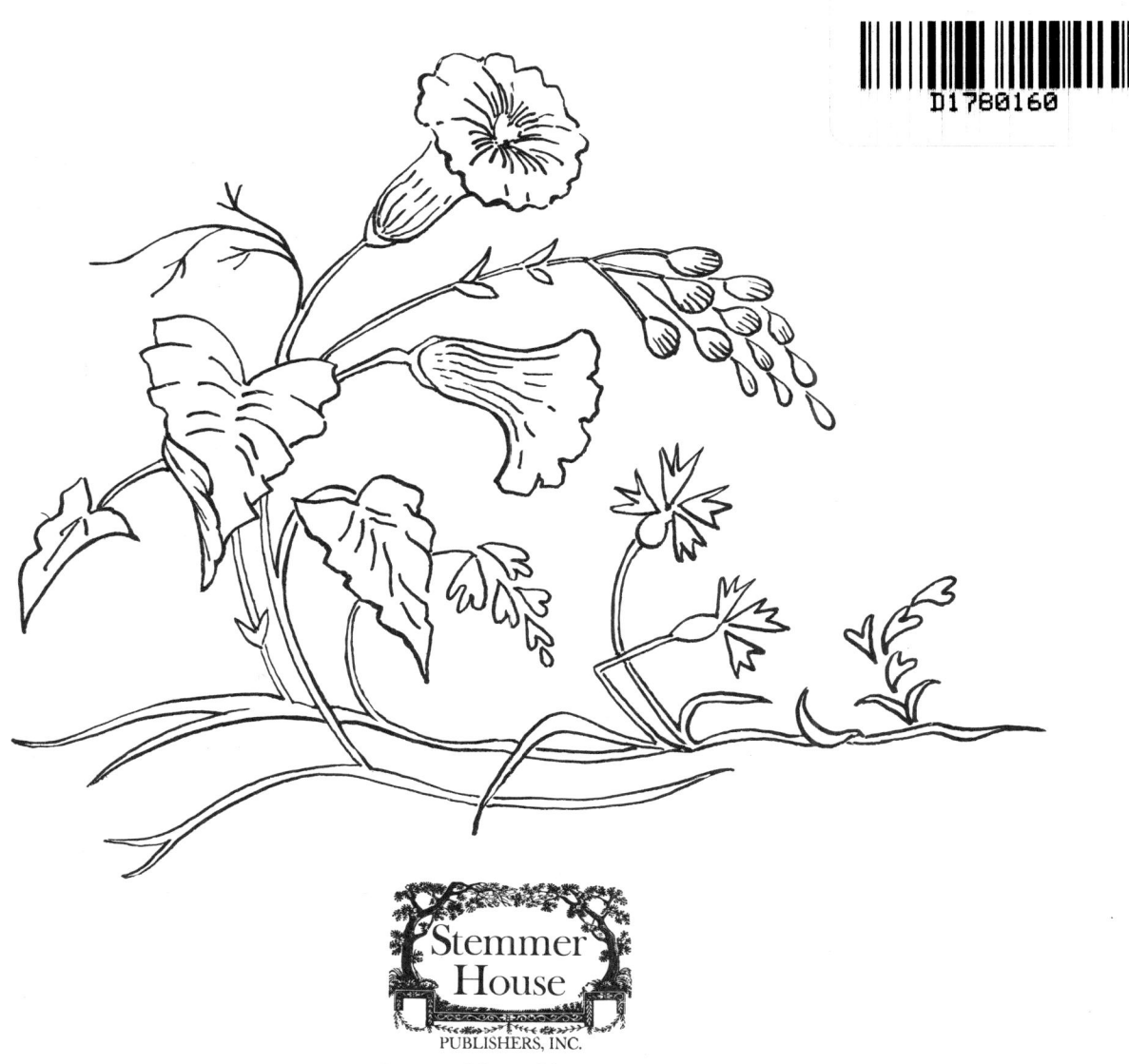

Stemmer House
PUBLISHERS, INC.
OWINGS MILLS, MARYLAND

Copyright © 1986 by Dolores M. Andrew

All rights reserved

All individual designs in this book may be used in any manner without permission. However, no grouping of 15 or more designs in a single collection for commercial purposes, and no part of the text may be used or reproduced in any manner whatsoever, electrical or mechanical, including xerography, microfilm, recording and photocopying, without written permission, except in the case of brief quotations in critical articles and reviews. The book may not be reproduced as a whole, or in substantial part, without permission in writing from the publishers.

Inquiries should be directed to
**Stemmer House Publishers, Inc.
2627 Caves Road
Owings Mills, Maryland 21117**

Printed and bound in the United States of America

First Edition

A Barbara Holdridge book

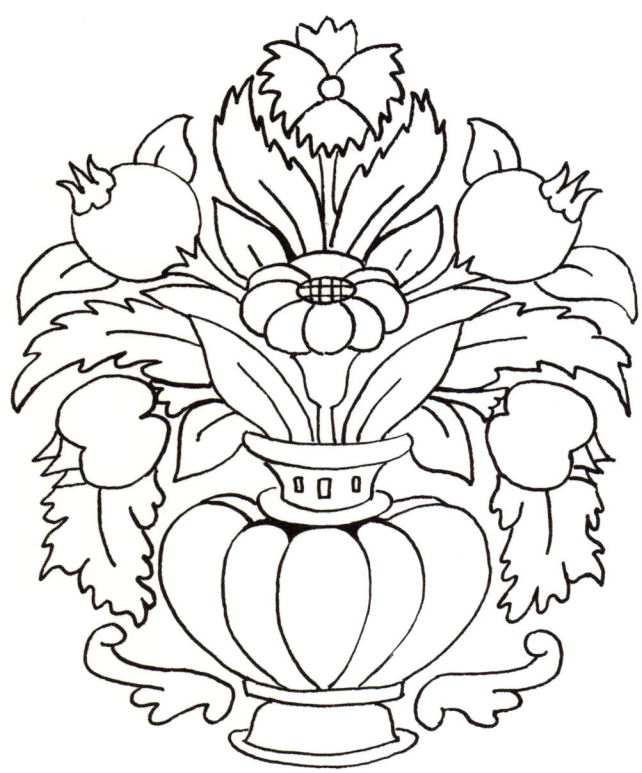

Dedication

To Rosemary Cornelius, who introduced me
to things Italian

Introduction

AT THE DAWN OF THE RENAISSANCE in the fourteenth century, Italy consisted of several small city-states. Those in the north were the most powerful. The Papal States covered much of the central area. The Renaissance flourished in the enlightened atmosphere of these city states — predominantly in Florence, Venice, Milan and Pisa. Ferrara and Genoa were also prominent for a time, but Venice and Florence remained leaders longer. All local governments encouraged and sponsored art and learning as part of their civic images. Each city-state had its own regional character, customs and traditions, including styles of art and textiles. These differences may have been influenced by geography, but were also defined by the politics of the city-state system.

Florence supported art and artists more generously than any other city-state, and artists were attracted to this environment. Besides its importance as a mercantile center, Florence became known for textiles. The technique of dye-making had been brought there from the East and was kept a carefully guarded secret, resulting in a monopoly that lasted for years. Florentine dyers could produce more values of any color than any competitor, enabling them to produce more variety in textiles, more interesting fabrics, and a wider range of colors of embroidery threads. The small towns around Florence developed distinctive embroidery techniques. For example, Casalguidi is a type of pulled thread work, and takes its name from the town near Florence. Lucca, near Pisa, was known for a special kind of gold work. Assisi gave its name to the distinctive cross-stitch embroidery in which the background is covered and the designed area is left blank. The Florentine stitch is one of the many names of the canvas stitch, known generally today as Bargello, which was inspired by one of the chair patterns in the Bargello Museum in Florence.

Venetians lived to glorify their city — built around 450 A.D. on 100 tiny islands in the Adriatic to escape Attila's raids. As natural seamen and merchants, they established trade with the Near East, introducing the riches found there to the markets of the West. Spices, textiles, jewels and lace were especially profitable. The Venetians not only bought and sold the lavish wares, but used them in their own costumes and furnishings. Textiles such as silk, brocade, velvet and lace often were further embellished with embroidery done in silk, metal threads or glass beads.

Metal thread for embroidery was another product made by a secret method in the Orient, until it was discovered and stolen by Byzantine traders. Venetians stole it in turn, introducing the methods and materials to Europe during the Crusades. Lace-making was also learned by Venetians in their travels. It became not only a fashion accessory in the High Renaissance, when elaborate collars and ruffs were worn, but an important international trade commodity. The wife of a doge sponsored a lace school, which inspired a continual interest in this art; a similar school still exists there today. The Venetians stole and plundered, but they also shared.

Several other regions had special textile techniques. Bologna was noted for a whitework, which is white embroidery on white linen or muslin fabric. This technique combines drawn work, cut work, needleweaving and some surface embroidery. The embroidery derives its interest from the textures created by the various stitches.

Perugian textiles are distinctive in character and date from the twelfth century. Usually woven on a birdseye type fabric in a dark blue cotton thread, they were often depicted as altar cloths in Renaissance paintings. For example, in Leonardo's famous painting of the Last Supper, and in Ghirlandaio's lesser known work of the same subject, the patterned tablecloths are Perugian designs.

Sicily was a thriving center for textiles as early as the twelfth century, when conquering Saracens taught weaving to the natives. The areas around Palermo became known for outstanding brocade, velvet and silk. One of the best known and oldest examples of this work is the coronation mantle of the Norman king Roger II. In regular use from 1220 until the nineteenth century, it was worn at coronations of the Holy Roman Emperors. It features two symmetrical, stylized lions in blue silk, outlined in pearls, on a scarlet silk ground, and is now preserved now in a museum in Vienna.

The main outlet for elaborate embroidery among most of the peasant class was the native costume. The costumes vary from dark, heavy somber fabrics in the north to light and more showy fabrics and colors in the south. Women's bodices and aprons were usually trimmed with ribbon, lace or embroidery. Often the bodice had removable sleeves to allow the woman to work while wearing the costume.

Men's costumes were plainer but did have ribbon or feather decorations and were made from the same serviceable fabric as that worn by women. Head coverings of one kind or another were popular, especially in the colder regions. Favorite colors were blue and green as well as red, which was usually worn only at weddings. Many techniques were popular for embellishing peasant clothing, but embroidery was used only where it showed.

Textiles in the Renaissance served various purposes. The most important textiles in household furnishings were the bed hangings, since the bed was the most important piece of furniture in the home. Every home, no matter how modest, had bed hangings, and they were usually embroidered.

The other major use of textiles was for apparel. Sumptuary laws, which regulated personal expenditures and habits on moral and religious grounds, attempted to control clothing embellishment in many localities. However, many ignored these regulations, and the use of embroidery to decorate clothing was still widely practiced. Because of their income level, the lower classes were most affected by these laws.

The clothing of the wealthy was ornate. Long flowing robes and high headdresses of the early Renaissance gave way to elaborate doublets, hose, high collars and bejewelled gowns. With embellishment almost an obsession, even velvet was sometimes embroidered or covered with jewels, stitched with a single thread. The ornate clothes were heavy and cumbersome, but style, not comfort, prevailed. Most of the embroidery was done with silk and metal threads in gold, silver or jewels. Wool was used only in tapestries and in canvas embroidery. Linen was used as a surface for embroidery and sometimes as a fine thread in lace making. Lace was also made from silk and cotton.

The diversity of Italian textiles and embroidery show the use of many stitches and techniques. However, only lace seems to be common to all regions, and even that varies in character from place to place. Lace in the Genoa area is rounded and geometric; in Venice it has a lighter, more intricate appearance. Lace done in rural regions is coarser than that in the more sophisticated city-states.

Subject matter for textiles, primarily wall hangings, became diverse during the Renaissance. The plain backgrounds behind pictures of Biblical events gradually developed into landscapes and pastoral scenes. Allegories and military deeds were popular for tapestries, and important citizens were depicted. Occasionally the patron was shown in the allegory or military scene, thereby increasing his status through such glorification. In ecclesiastical textiles, Biblical scenes prevailed, but portraits of saints and the Virgin were also popular. Most of the textiles in the church were vestments and altar hangings, although some tapestries were also used.

There is some crudeness of technique evident in early Renaissance designs. Most later works, however, show great skill, a sense of detail and better modeling of figures. Folds fall naturally; the faces have character and expression. There is even some well-handled perspective. Many of these pieces were designed by Renaissance artists such as Botticelli, Raphael and Pollaiolo, and often similarity can be found between their embroidery designs and their paintings of the same subjects.

The Italian technique "Opus Italicum" was similar to "Opus Anglicanum," the English ecclesiastical technique of great skill and detail popular in the fourteenth and fifteenth centuries. Ecclesiastical designs were also done in "or nué," a Flemish technique which Italians used with great success. This involved couching — tacking down — gold thread with various colored threads, creating pictures of complex shading and great detail.

Media such as lace and counted thread do not lend themselves easily to realism in subject matter. Fabrics such as canvas, on which counted threadwork is done, use a squared ground treatment as does drawn thread, pulled thread and Assisi. Therefore, the designs used in these media were those which work best within these limitations — flowers, birds, animals, mottoes. Even so, the squares give a stylized character to any such design, because a "rounding" of any subject was difficult.

Most textiles designs of all kinds during the Renaissance favored floral motifs. Although many were done for secular use, floral designs frequently accompanied Biblical motifs on the same piece. During the early Renaissance, designs tended toward the heavy and gothic. In the fifteenth century, called "Quattrocento" by Italians to honor the Renaissance's golden age, the pomegranate theme was popular. It consisted of intertwined or interesting lines combined with other floral patterns. These forms continued to develop in the sixteenth century and became quite large, as was common in the artistic work of that period. Some designs tended toward geometrics, but were still stylized florals. The serpentine line became an "S" curve, which was sometimes combined with a rectangular shape, or "broken branch" motif. The two elements could be combined in countless arrangements: parallel, zigzag, alternating, etc., to create compositions of various shapes and combinations. When the textiles were used for apparel, the direction of the pattern was important, because horizontal lines are not flattering to most figures.

The "S" curve continued to dominate well into the next century, and faded in the mid-1600's as the subtly curved styles of the Baroque period developed. Designs based on a central "axis," with foliage curving almost to the sky, became predominant during the following years.

With the eighteenth century, other factors modified the character of Italian textiles. Developing trade with China influenced all European designs, and Italy was no exception. Elements of "Chinoiserie" were apparent in many motifs. Softer curves echoed the popularity of lace. The "S" curve and serpentine line reappeared as meandering patterns, again echoing the large floral motifs popular in the Rococo era. Toward the end of the century, striped patterns — which had enjoyed some popularity in the late sixteenth century —reappeared, enclosing the floral motifs. This could have been another manifestation of the "S" curve and "broken branch" themes which had sometimes been arranged horizontally, creating the striped effect.

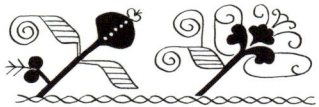

The use of color in Italian textiles developed as dyes improved. Red, green and white were popular during the early fifteenth century, and later variations of these colors were manufactured. Blue was rarely used until the seventeenth century, owing to the expense involved in making it. Gold and silver in metallic thread were used to accent patterns, as previously noted. In the sixteenth century, grounds used combinations of green, white and yellow, or of purple, white and yellow. Other variations were introduced for small motifs: olive, brown, wine. Many new colors were introduced in the seventeenth century, both light and dark: salmon pink, lime, turquoise, lemon, dark green, black, grey, dark brown.

Subtle colors appeared in the eighteenth century as the textile industry advanced even further. Lavish materials, combined with varied intricate designs, were typical of this century. Some textiles had a monochromatic theme of a bold color, but lightweight fabrics and pastel colors were popular, especially for feminine clothing.

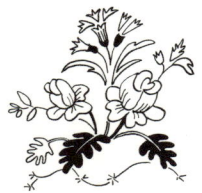

The designs in this book have been adapted from or inspired by various fragments of textiles. Some have come from brocades and velvets; others from Genoan lace, Perugian cottons, Sicilian borders or ecclesiastical vestments. Embroidered articles in Assisi, white work, silk and drawn work were also used.

When "collecting" became fashionable in the nineteenth century and textiles were found to have antique value, they were frequently cut into pieces by dealers, so that they could make more money from their sale. Unfortunately many valuable textiles were destroyed or ruined in this way, and we can now only guess at the original complete design, shape or use, from the remaining pieces.

Italian Renaissance textiles had a sophistication in both style and design. They were detailed and convoluted, filling every space; and even the negative space, the areas between the elements, was considered. Usually they were symmetrically balanced. If an element went left, there was a matching one to the right. Even if the design went in all four directions, symmetry prevailed. There were a few abstract designs in the modern sense, but even these were made up of recognizable elements.

Renaissance life was precarious, even dangerous. Towns and borders changed hands frequently in the almost constant wars. Death and disease were ever present. In art and design the Renaissance citizen found symmetry and a sense of order which was otherwise lacking in everyday life.

D.M.A.

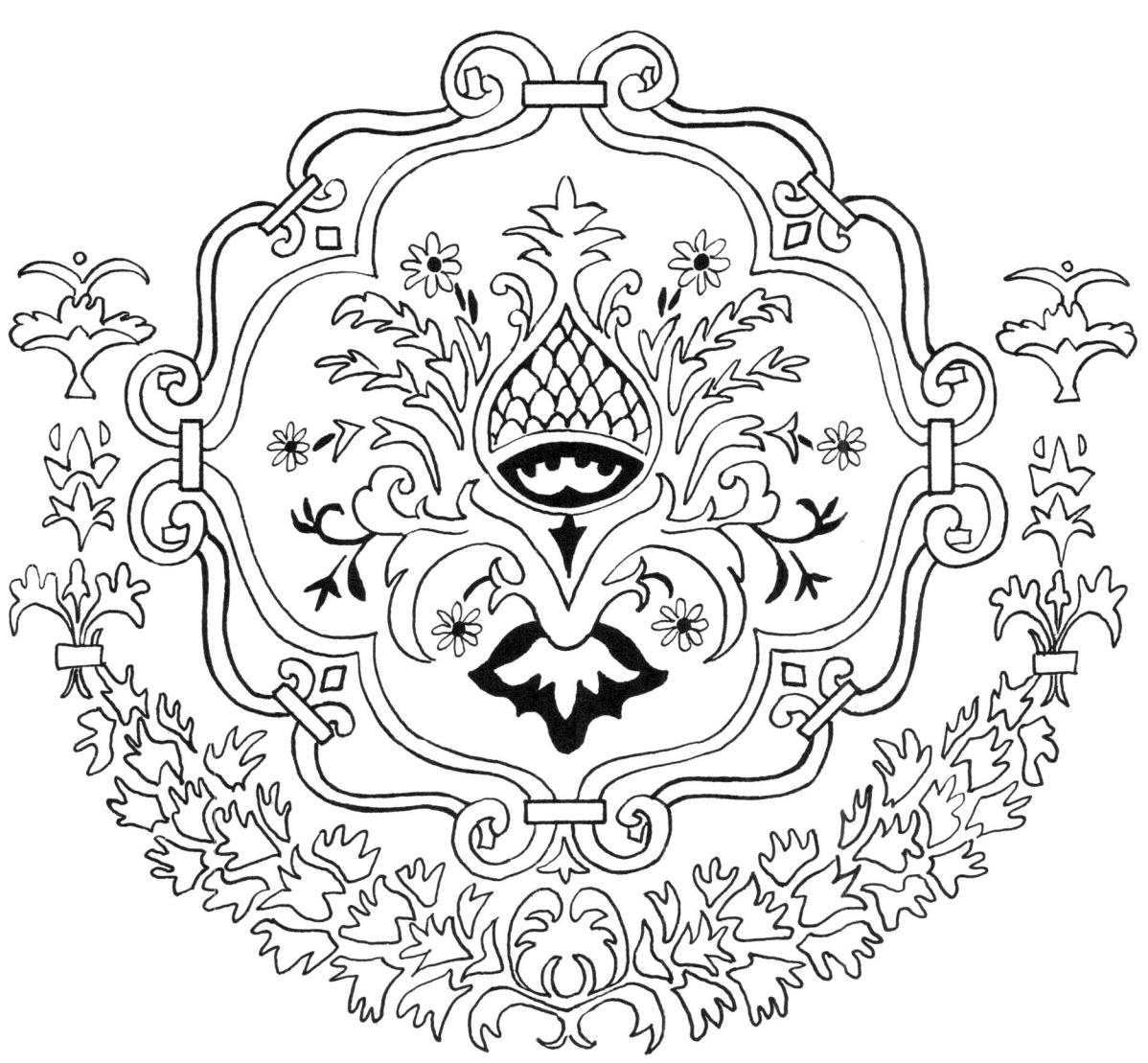

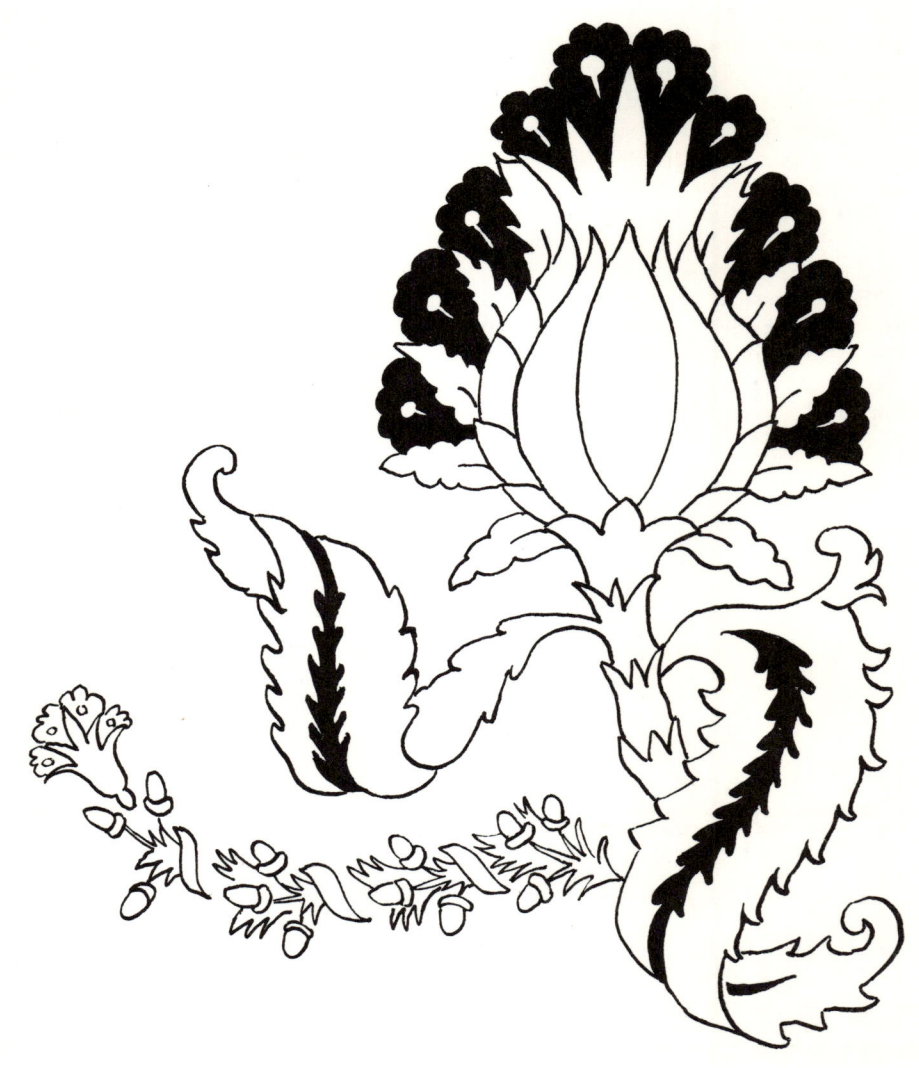
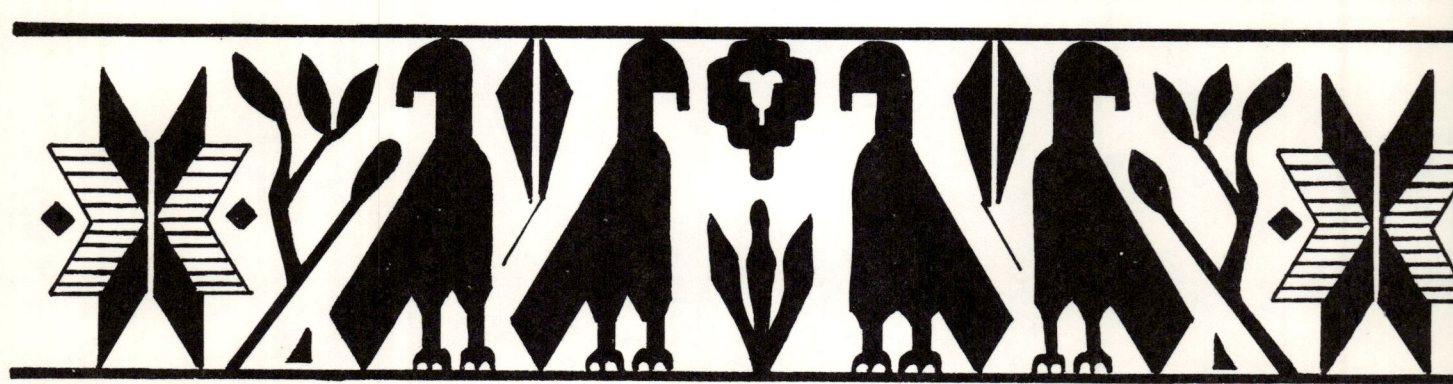

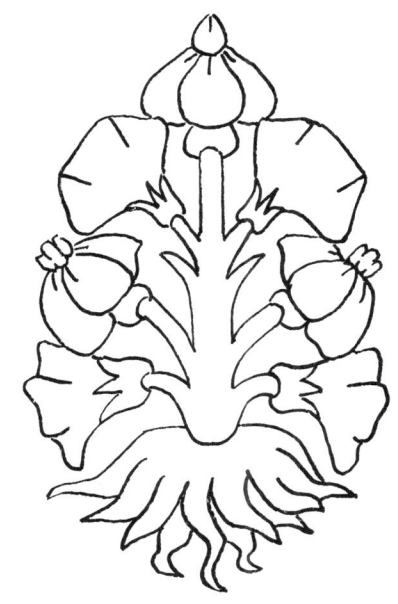

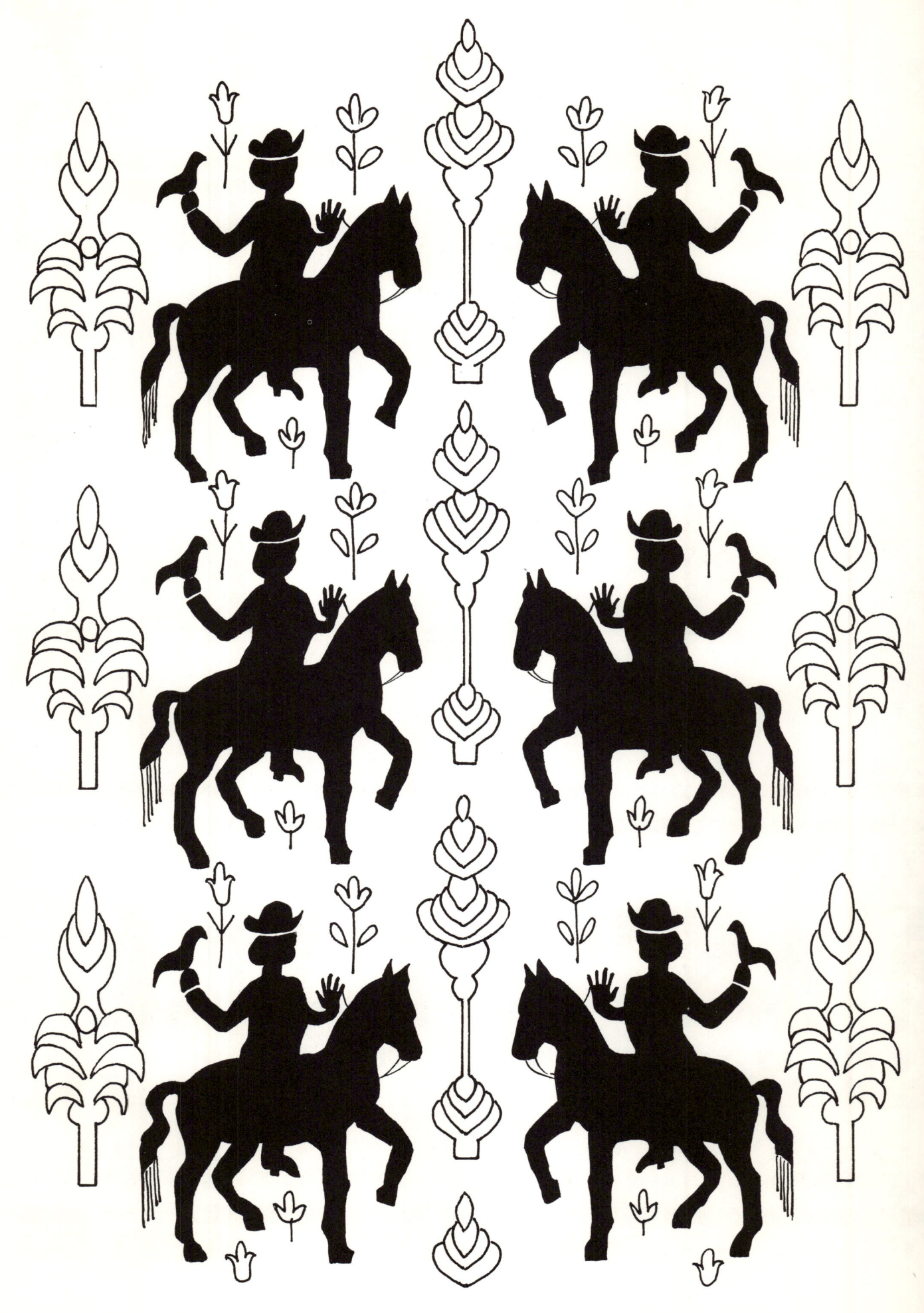

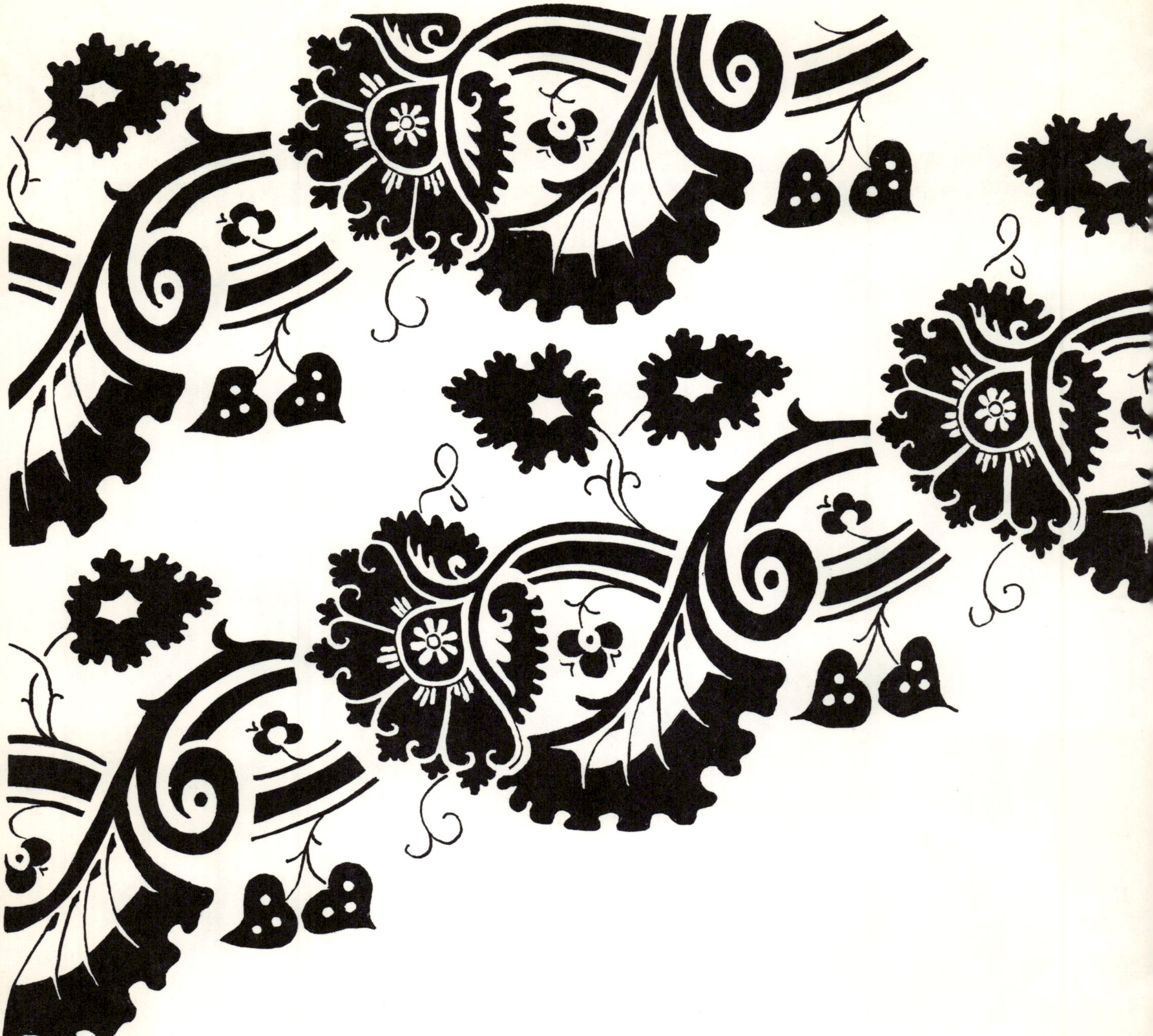

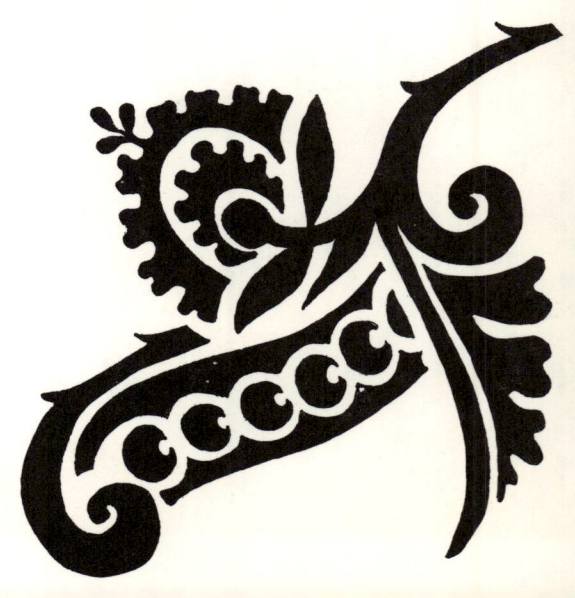

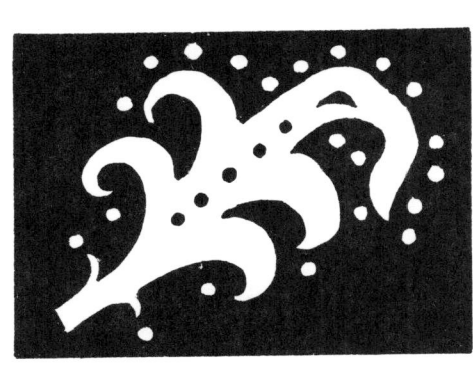

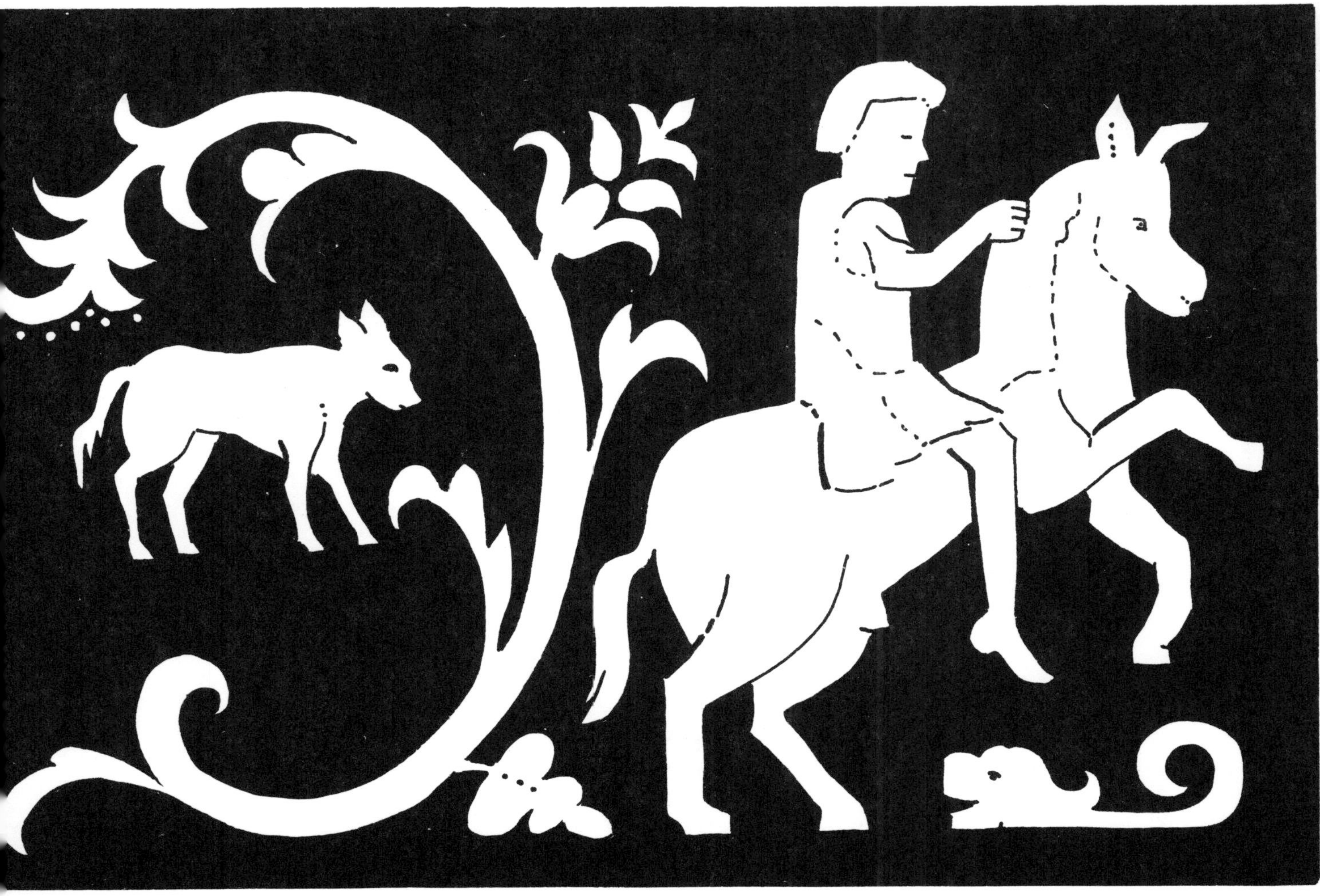

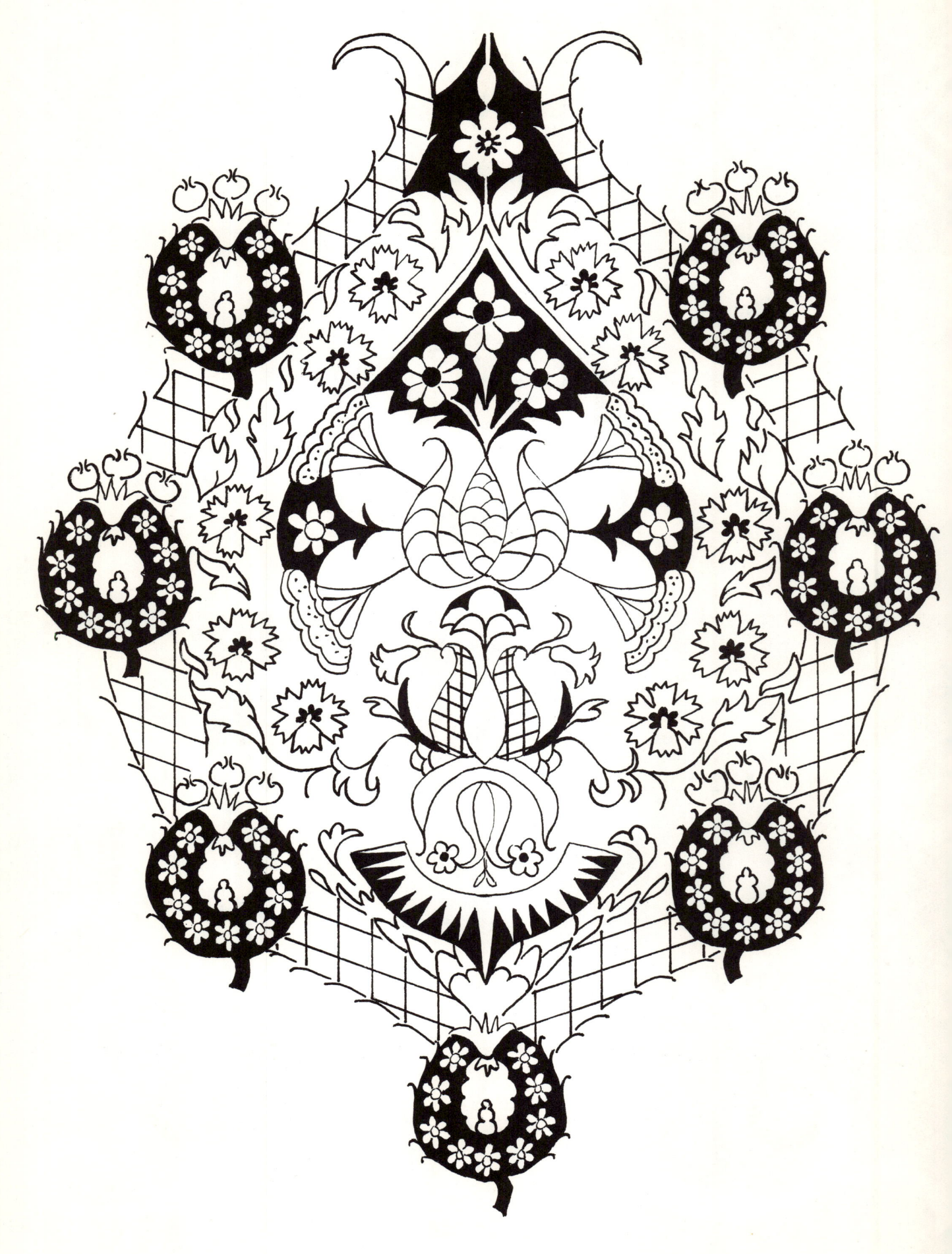

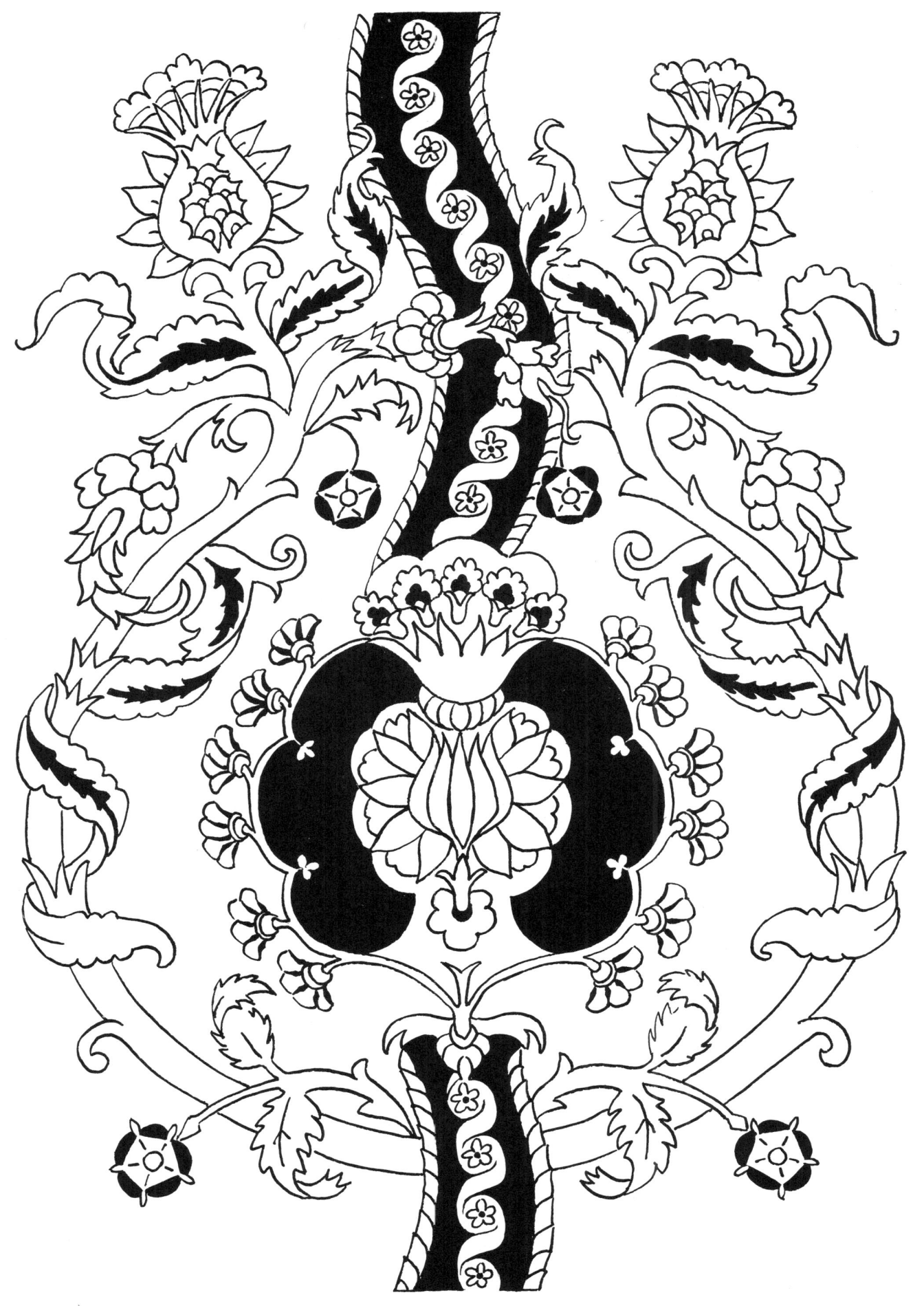

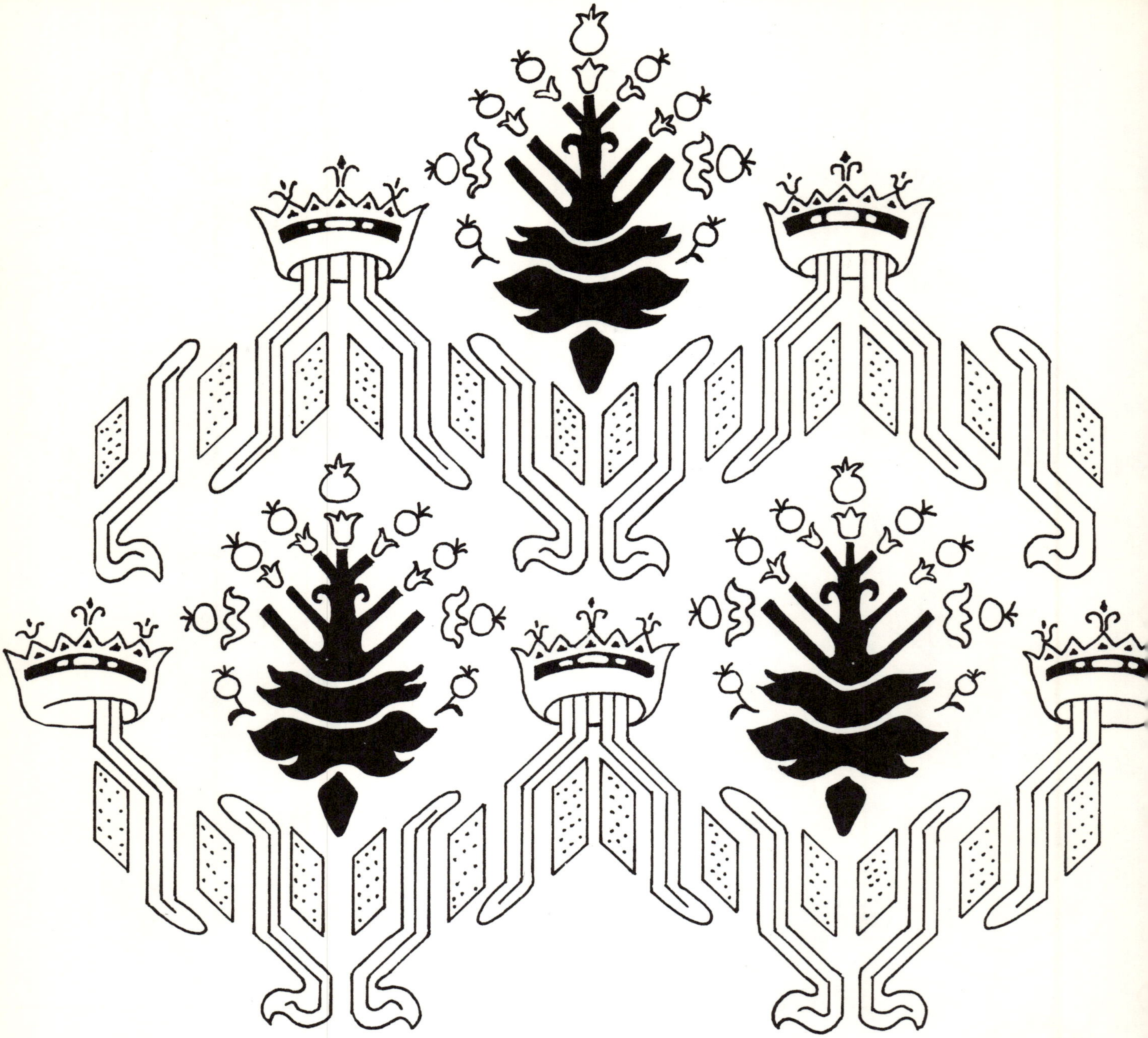

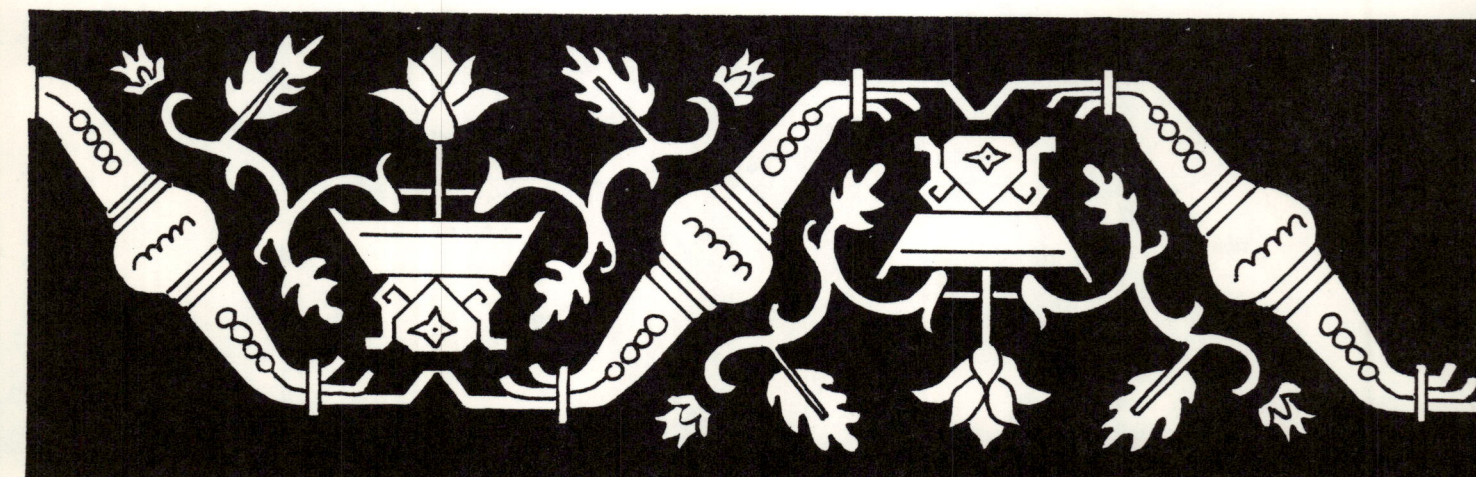

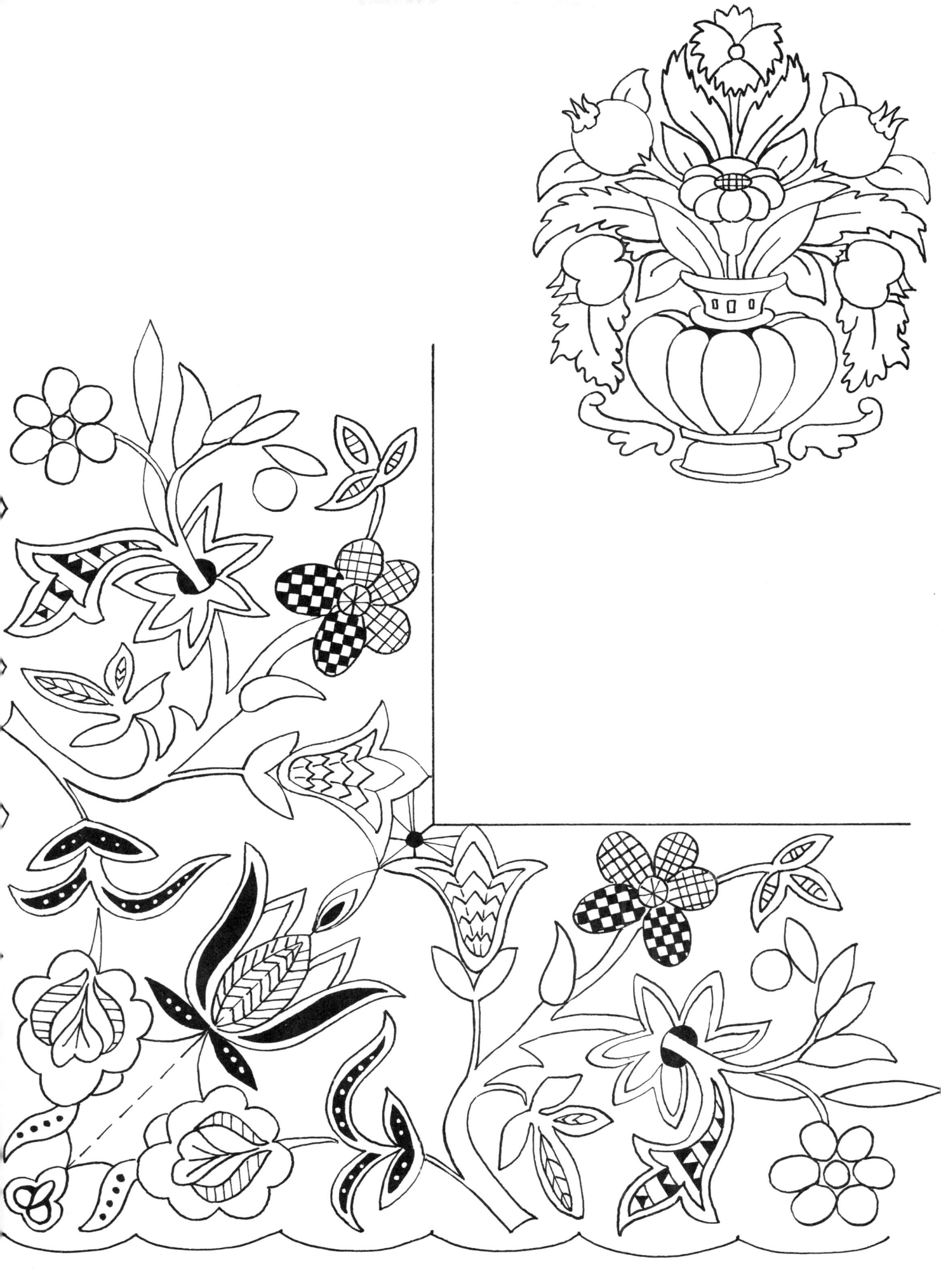

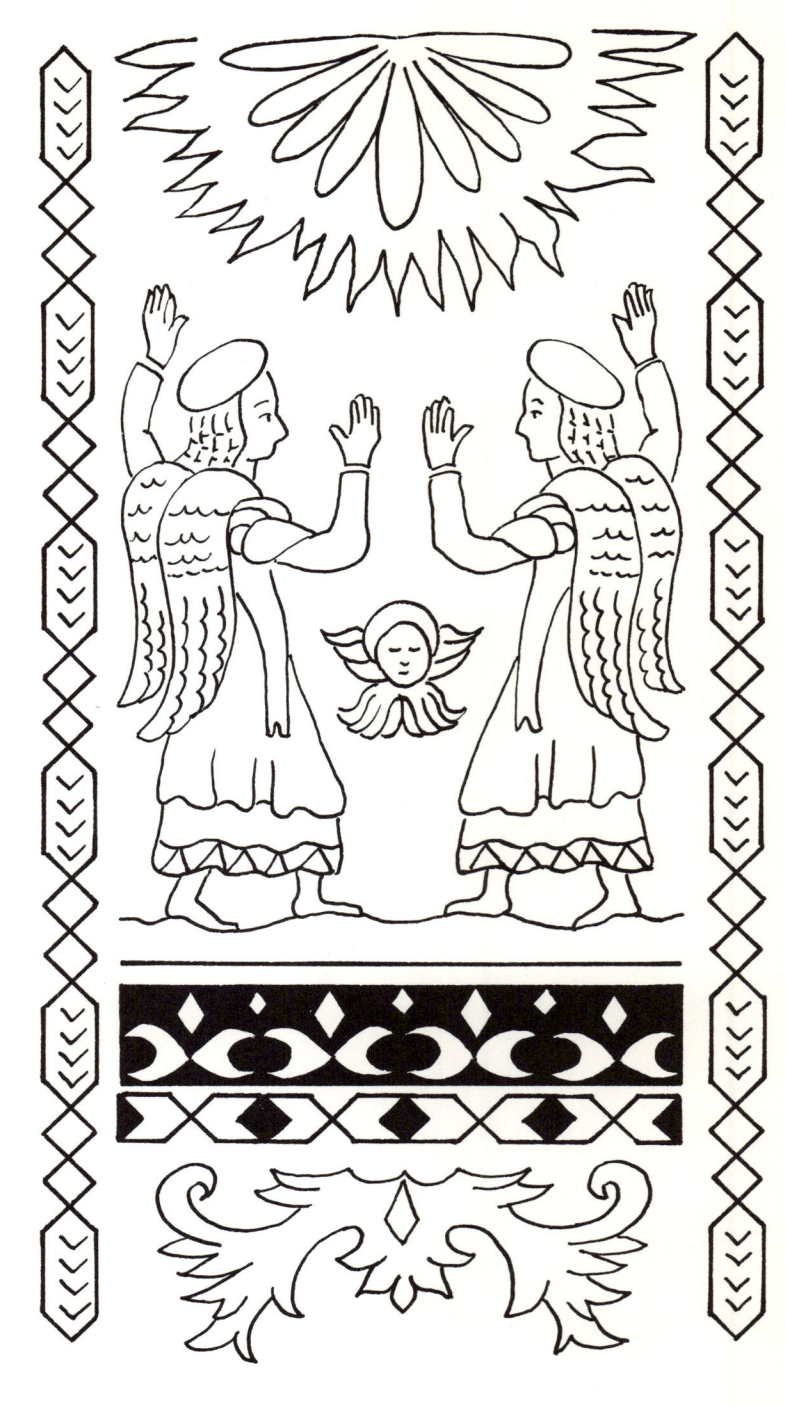

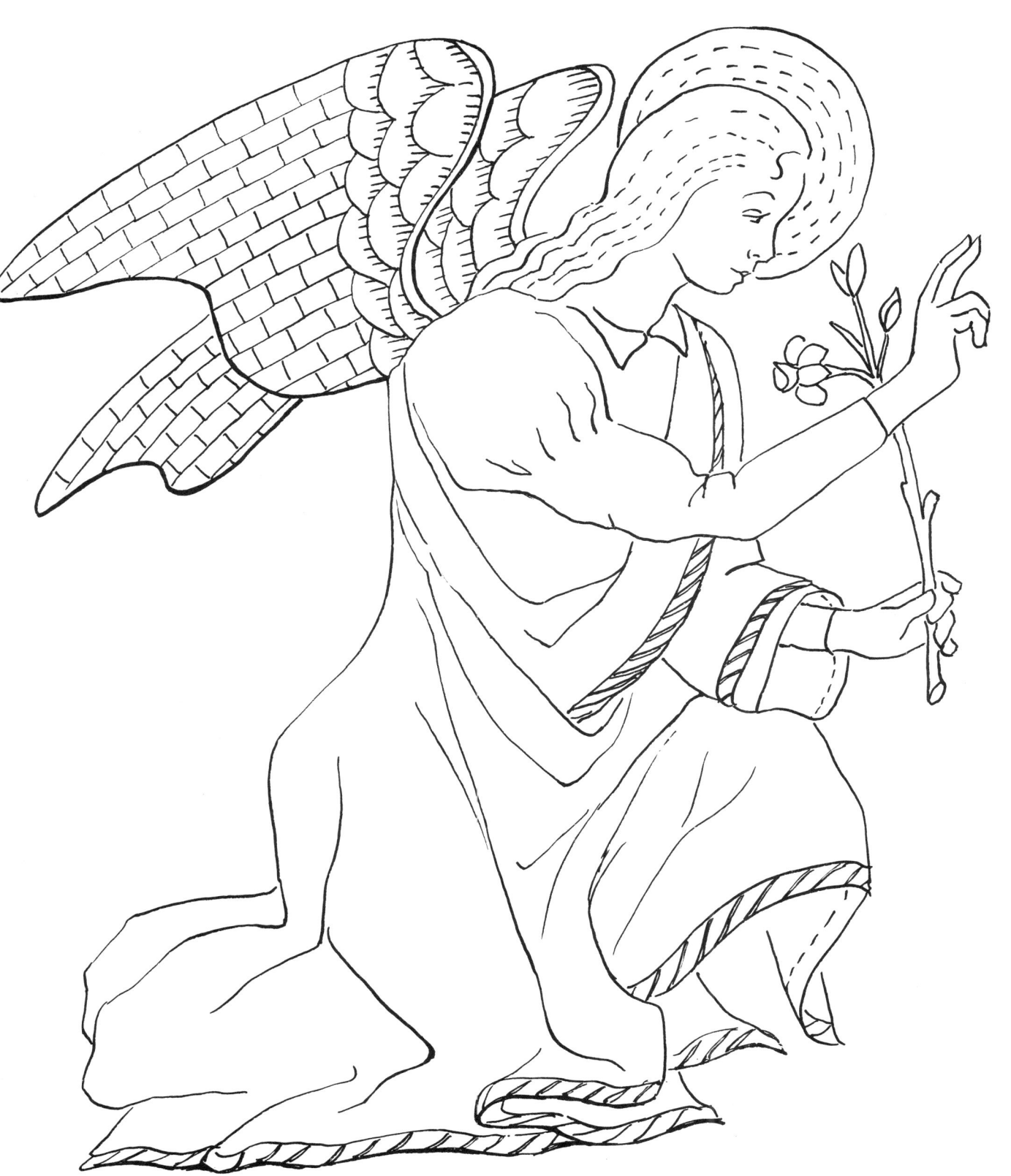

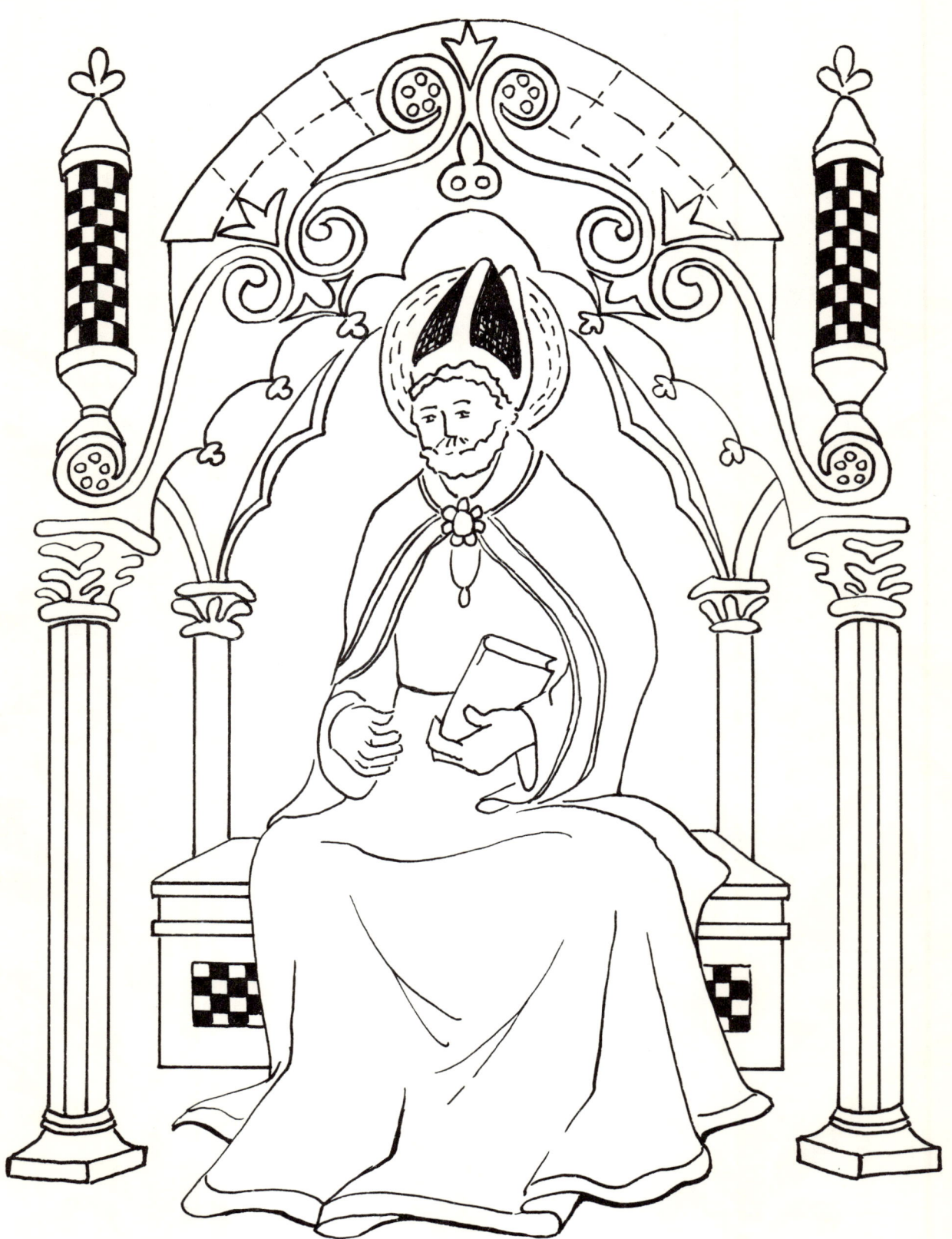

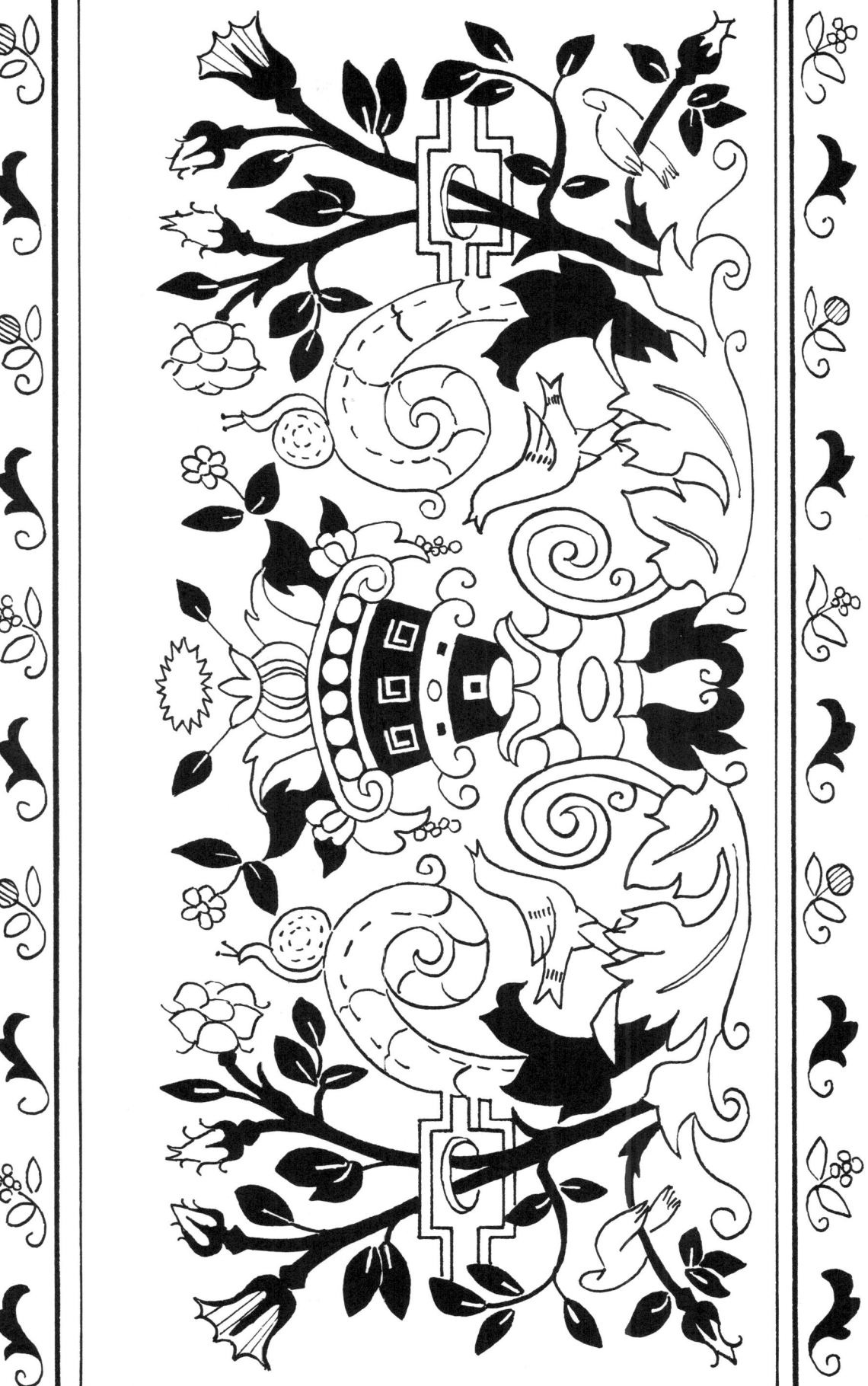

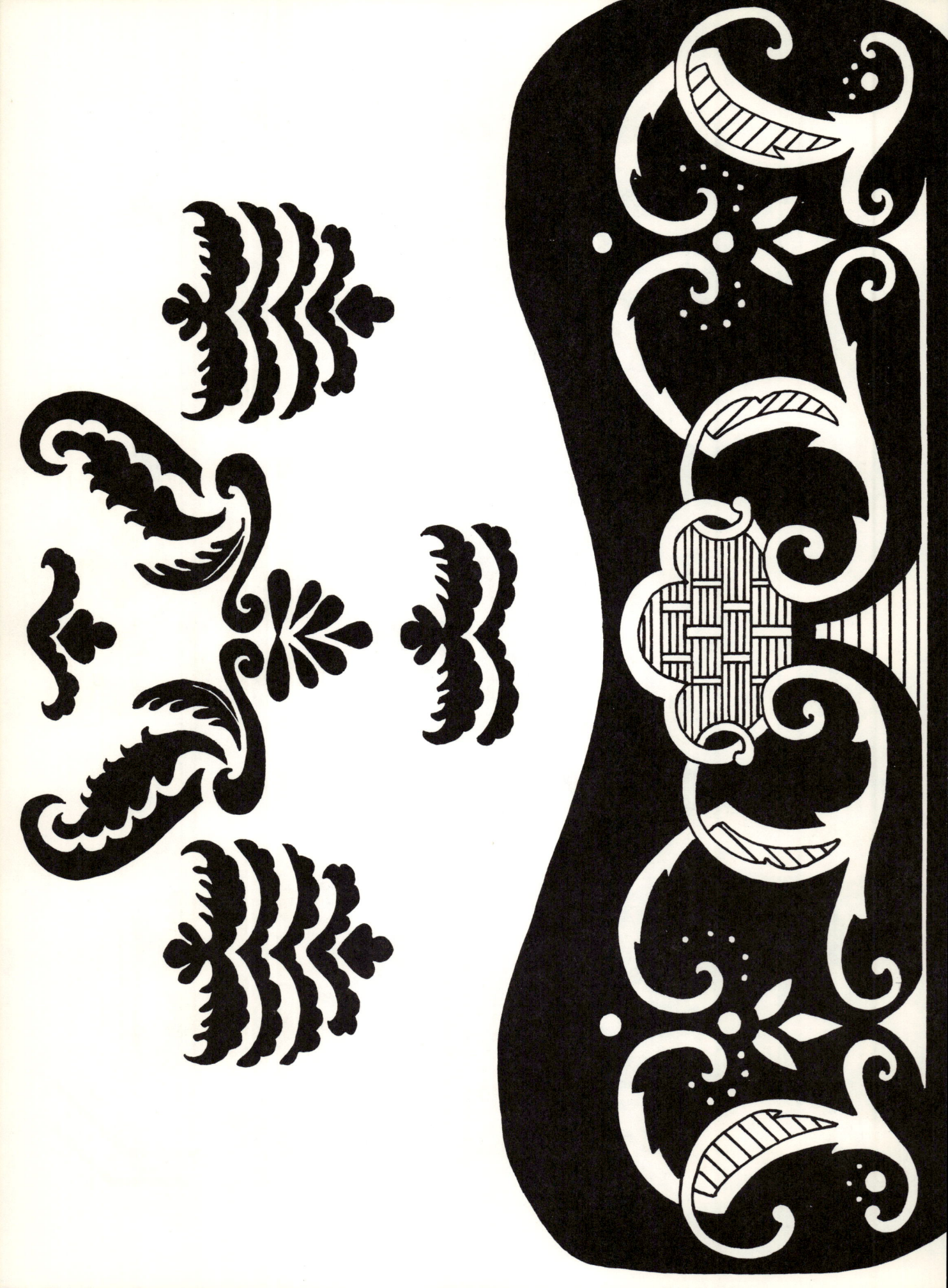

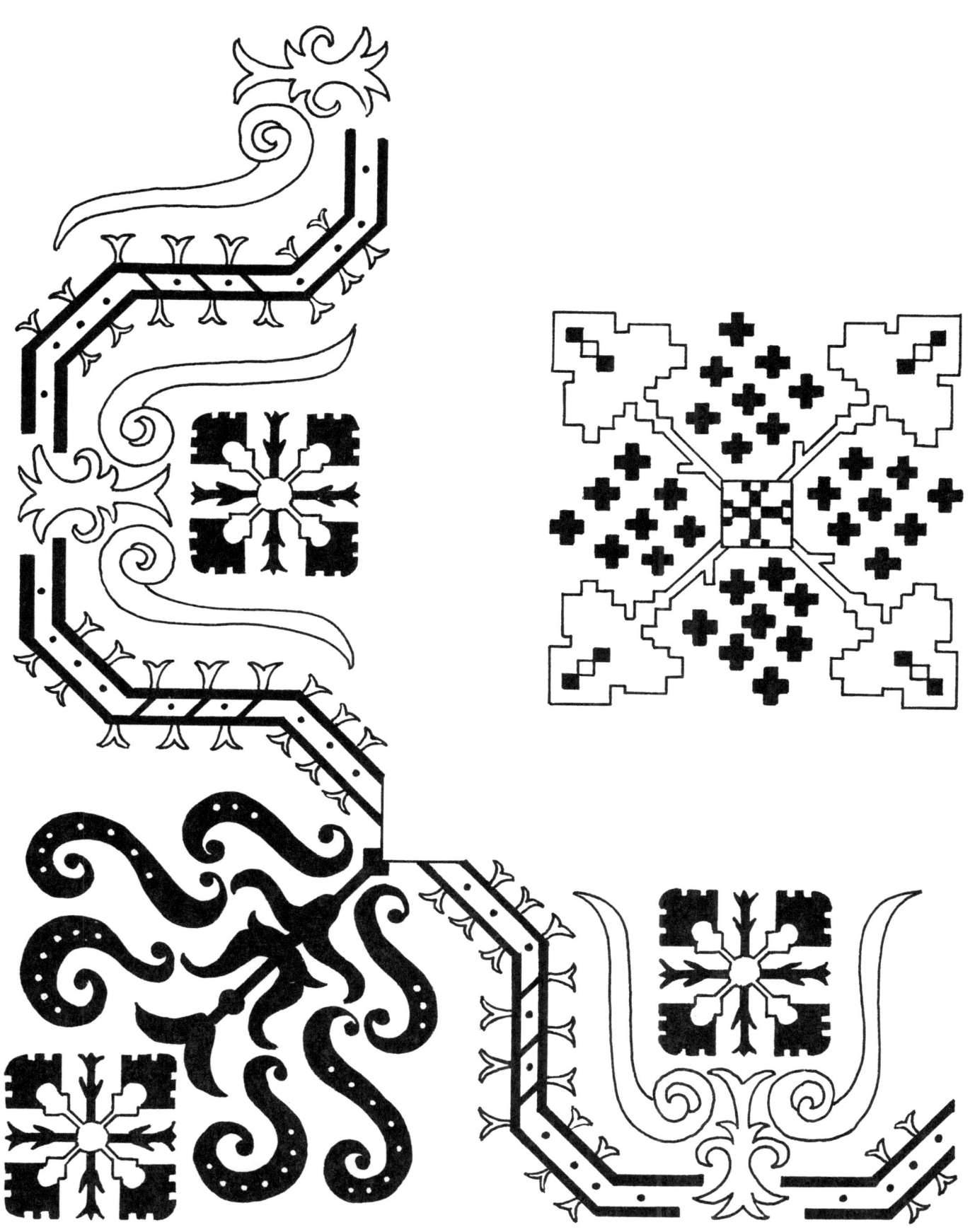

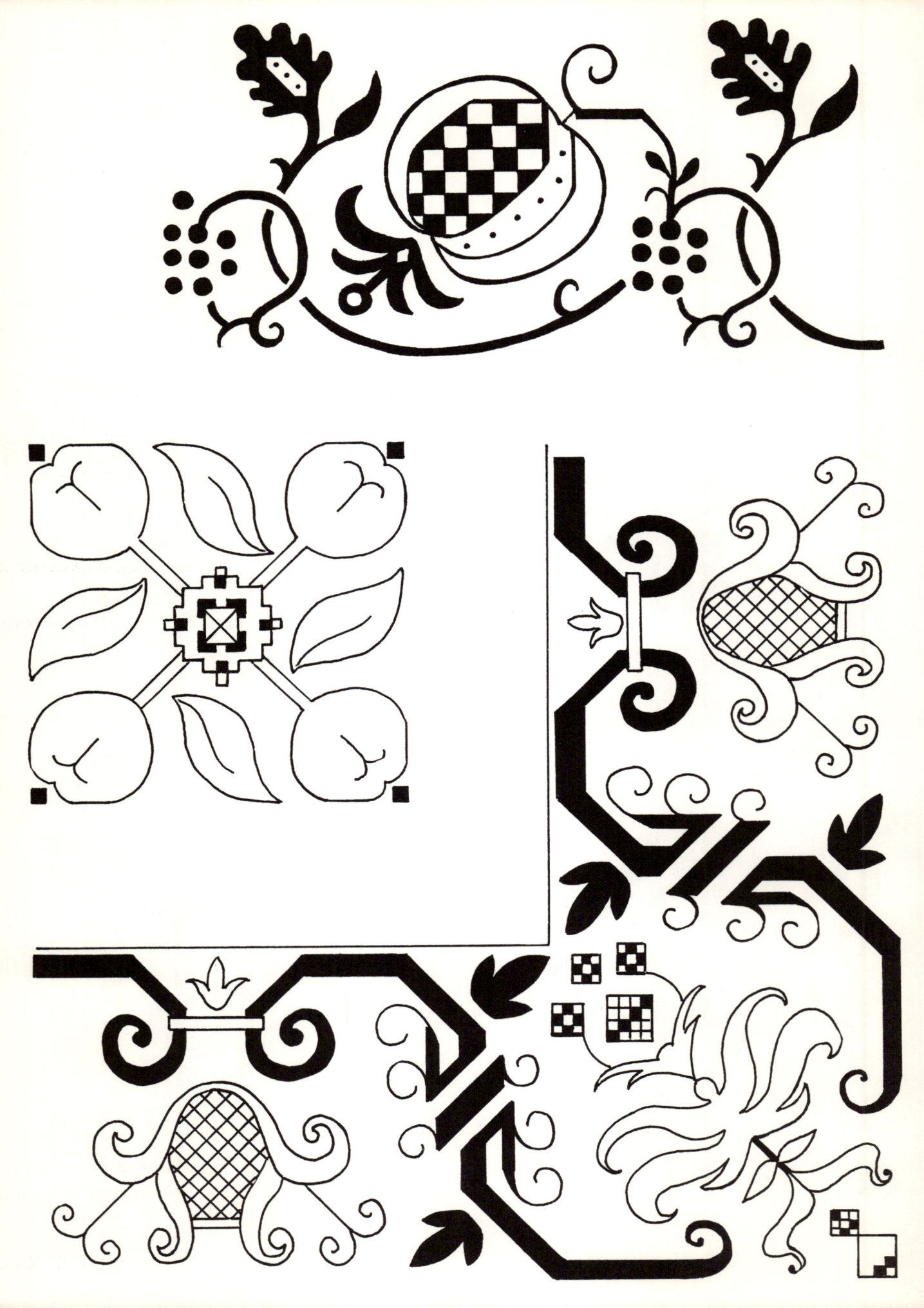

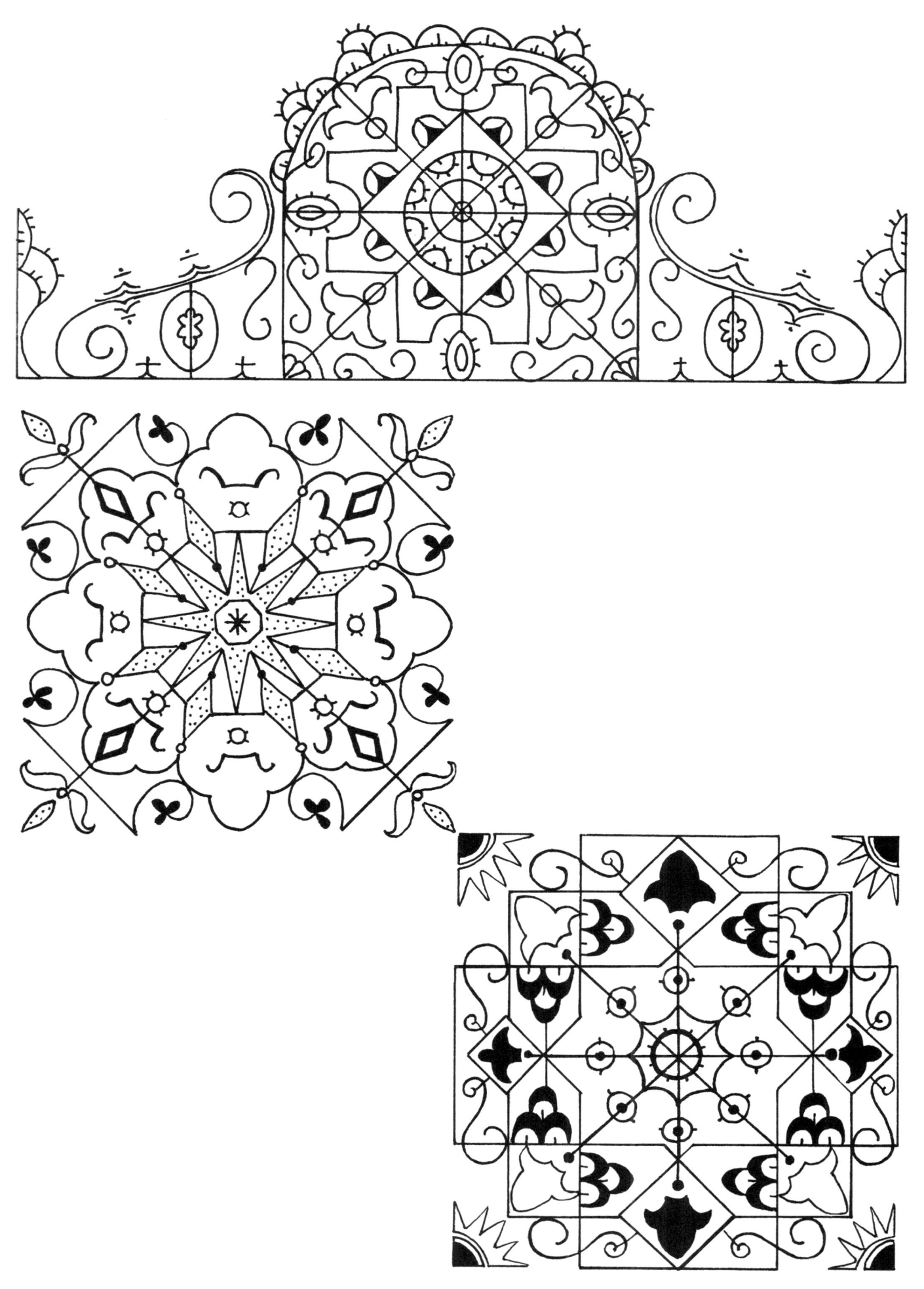

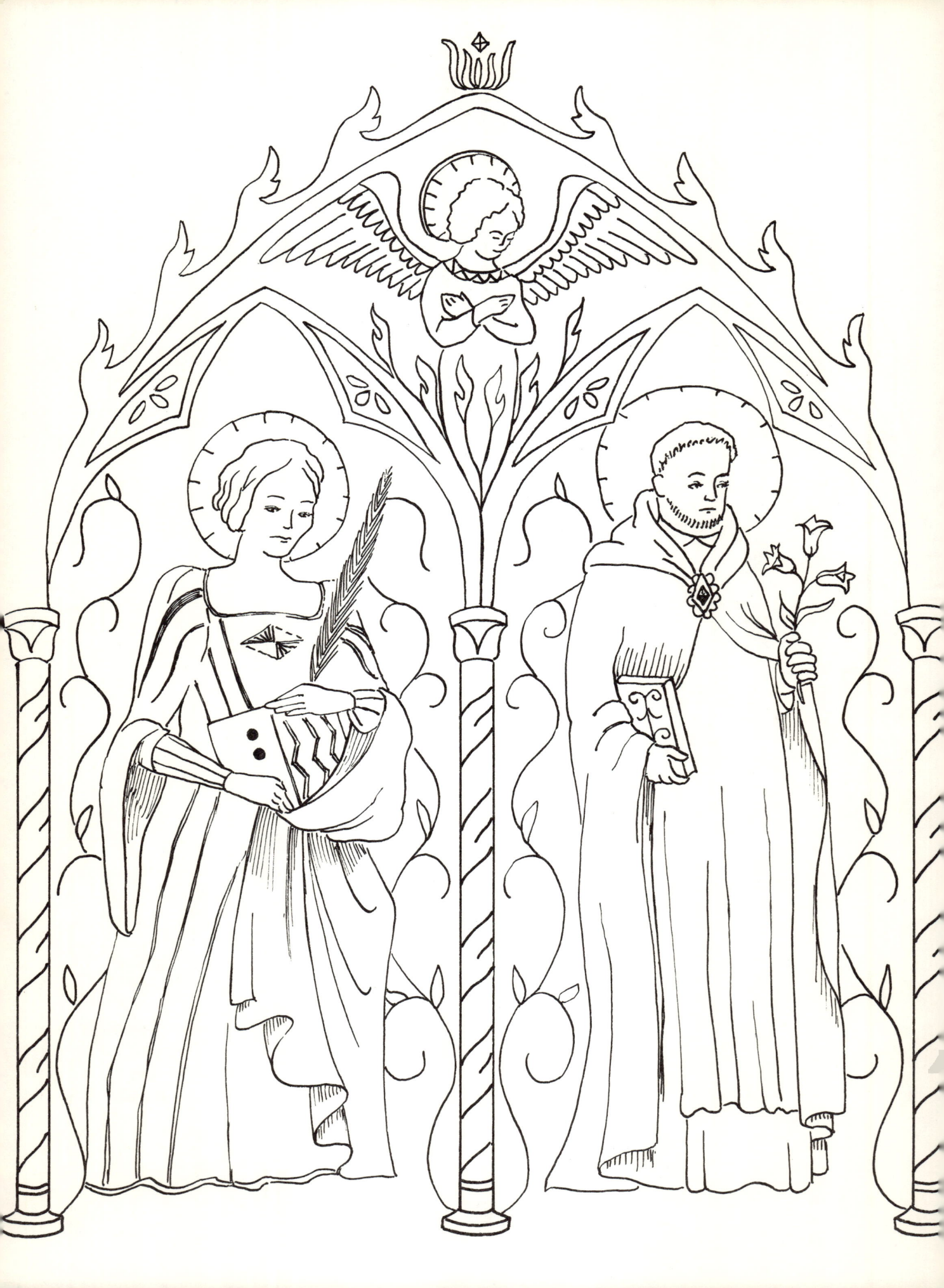

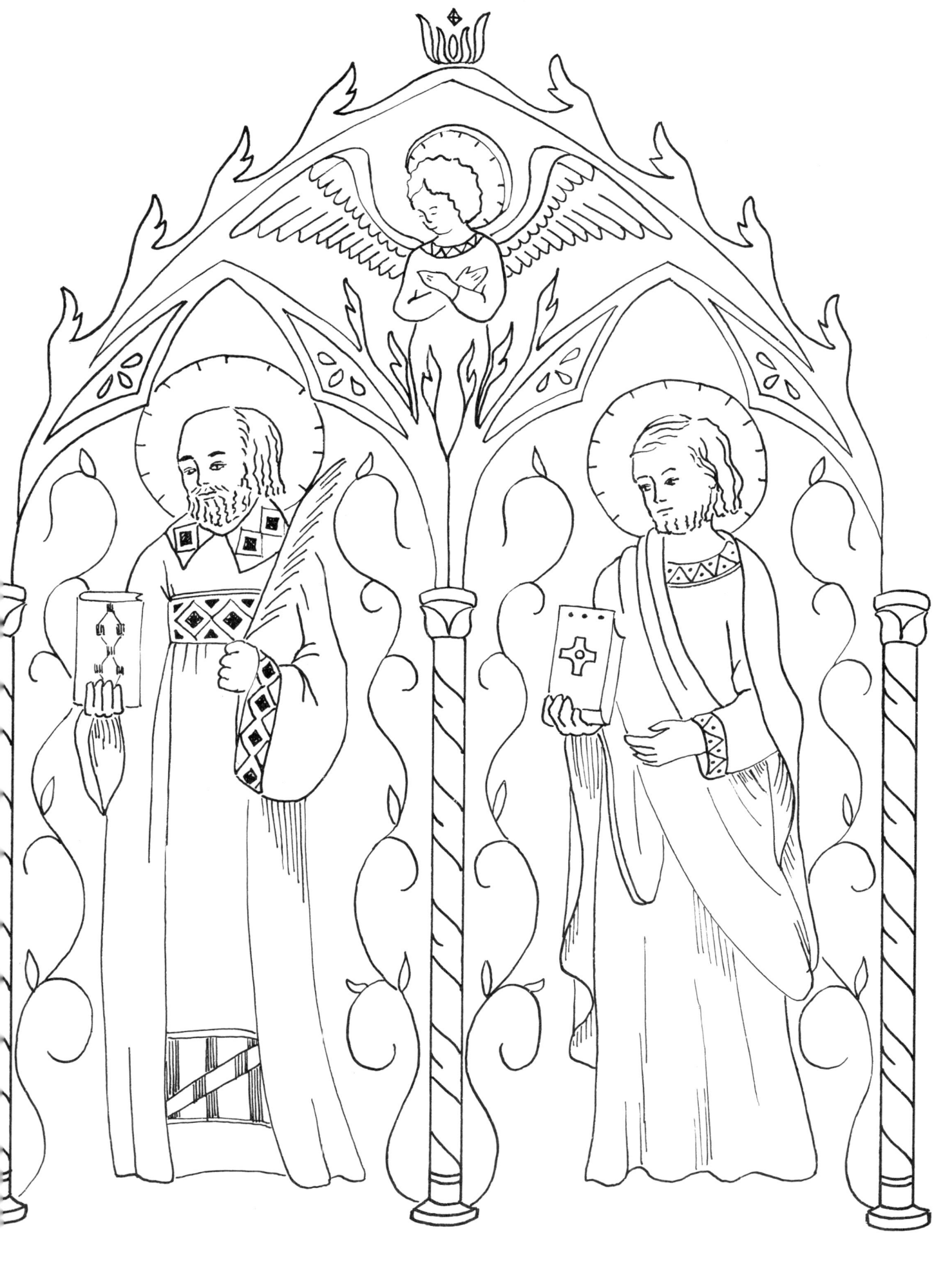

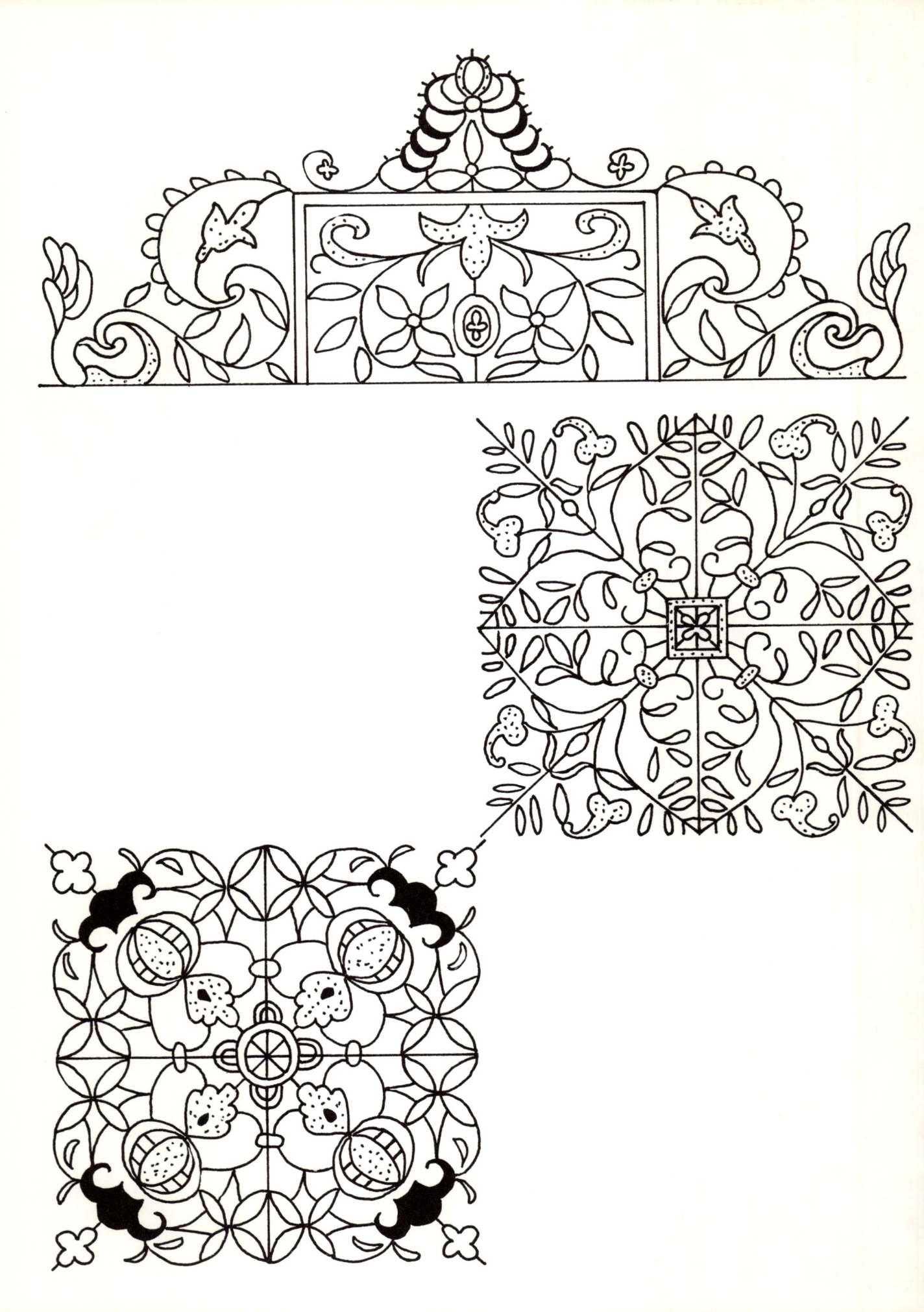

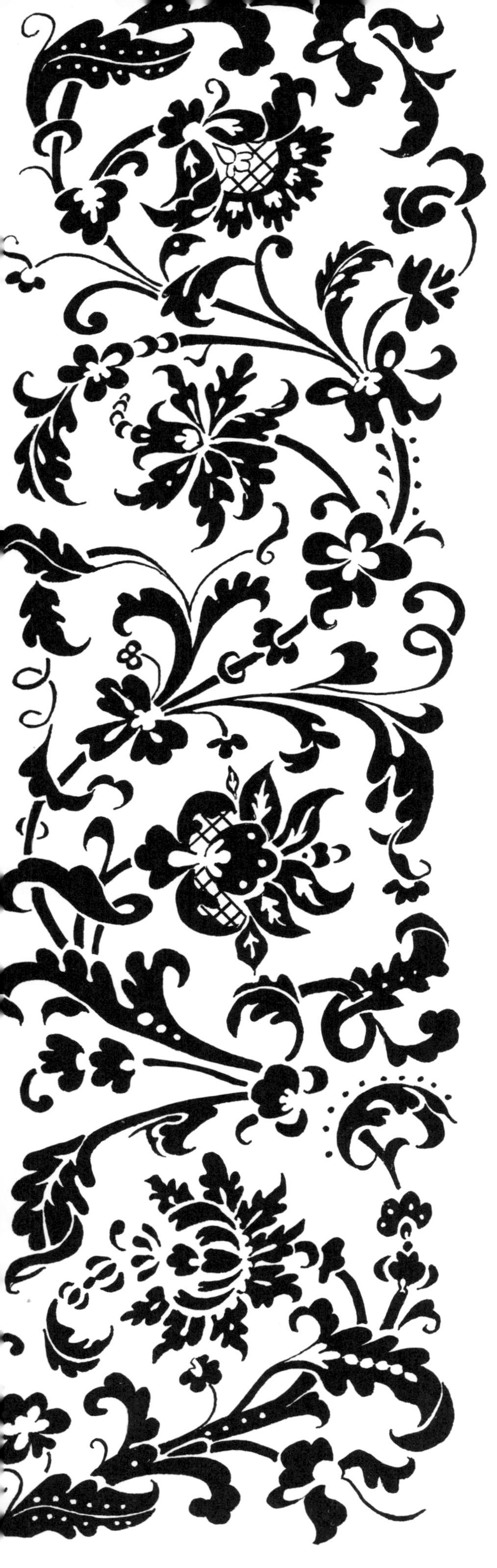

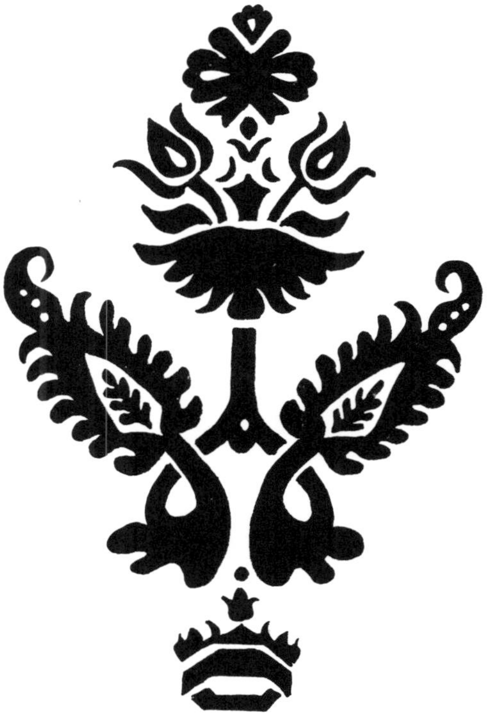

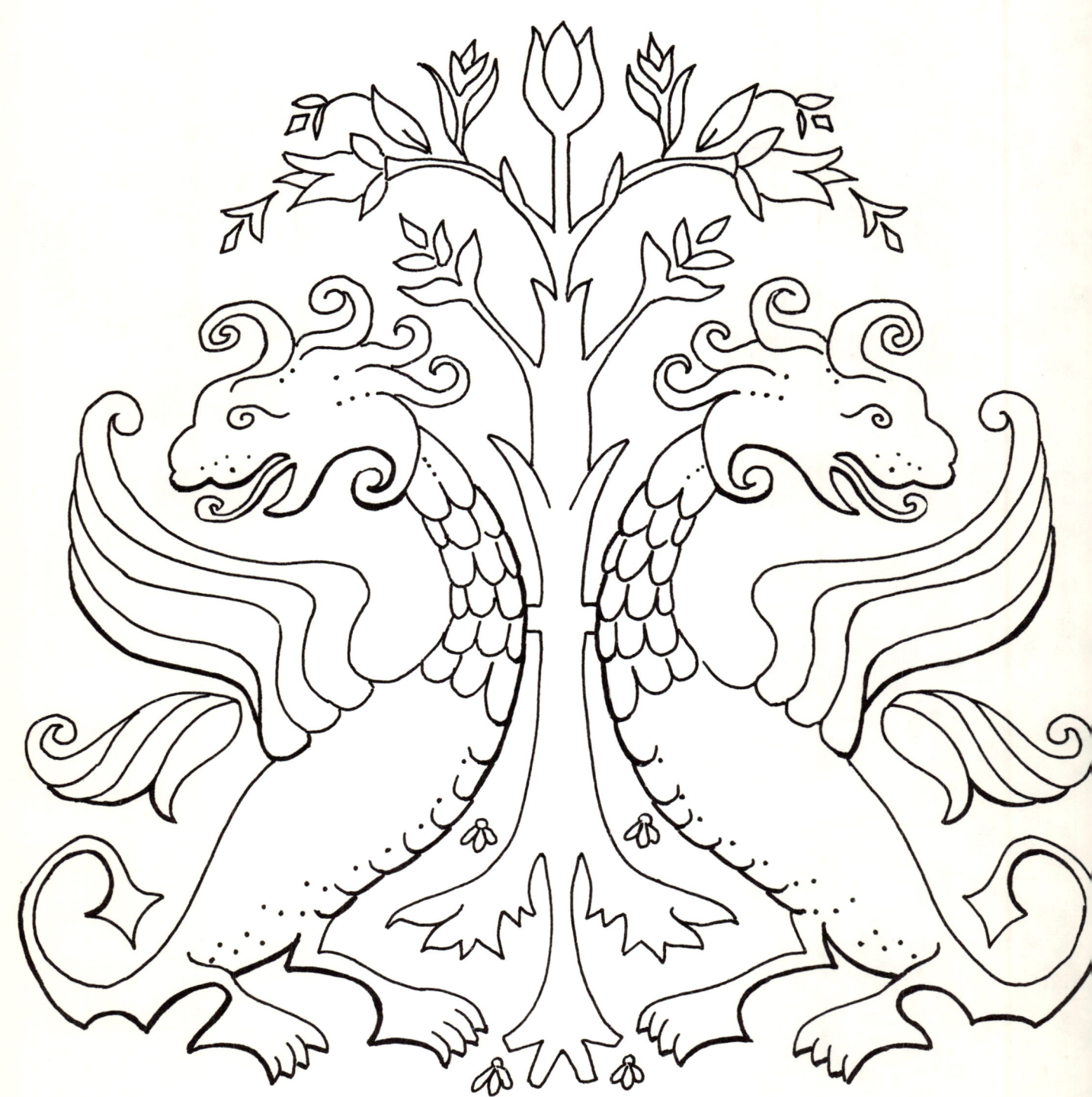

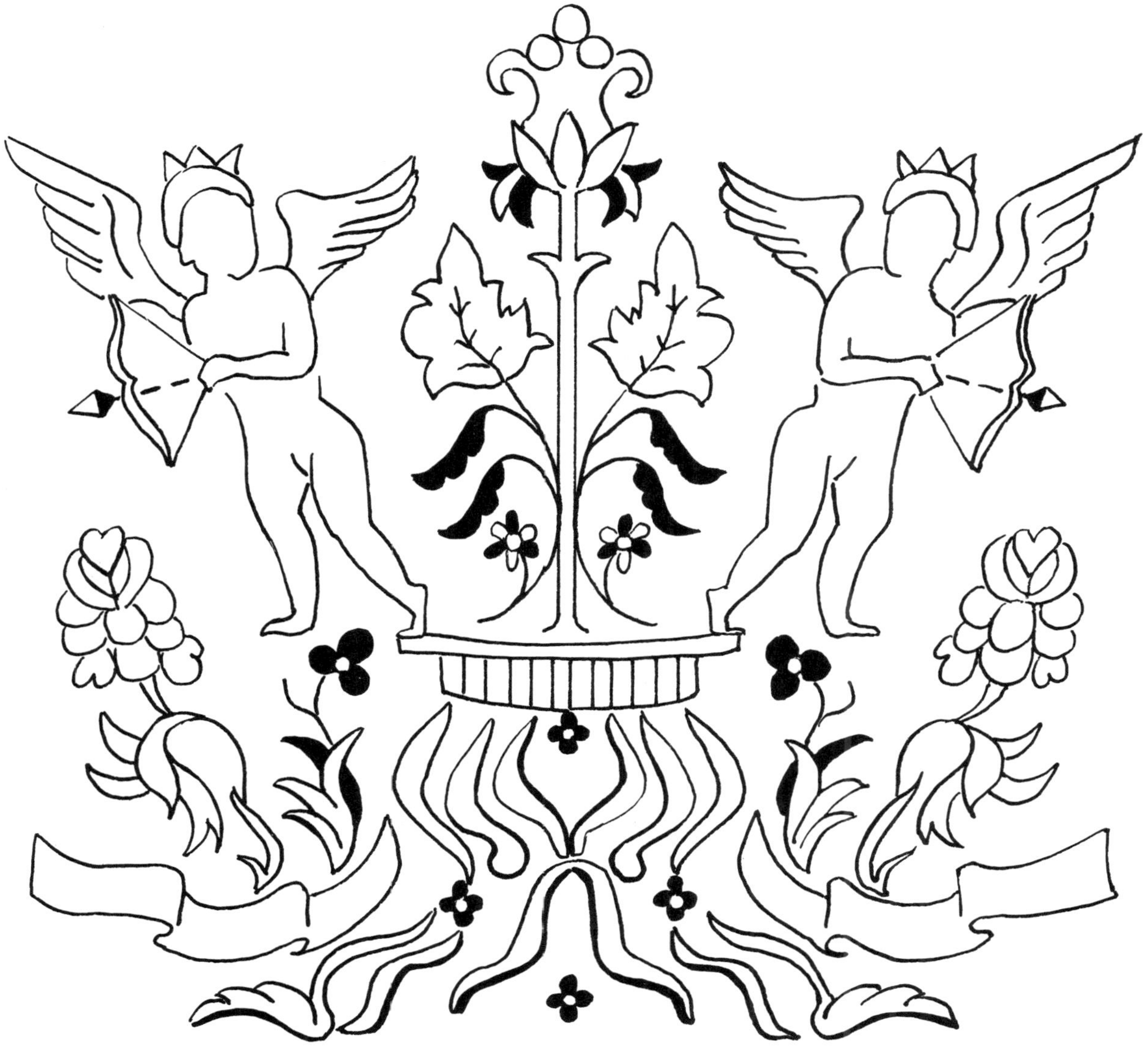

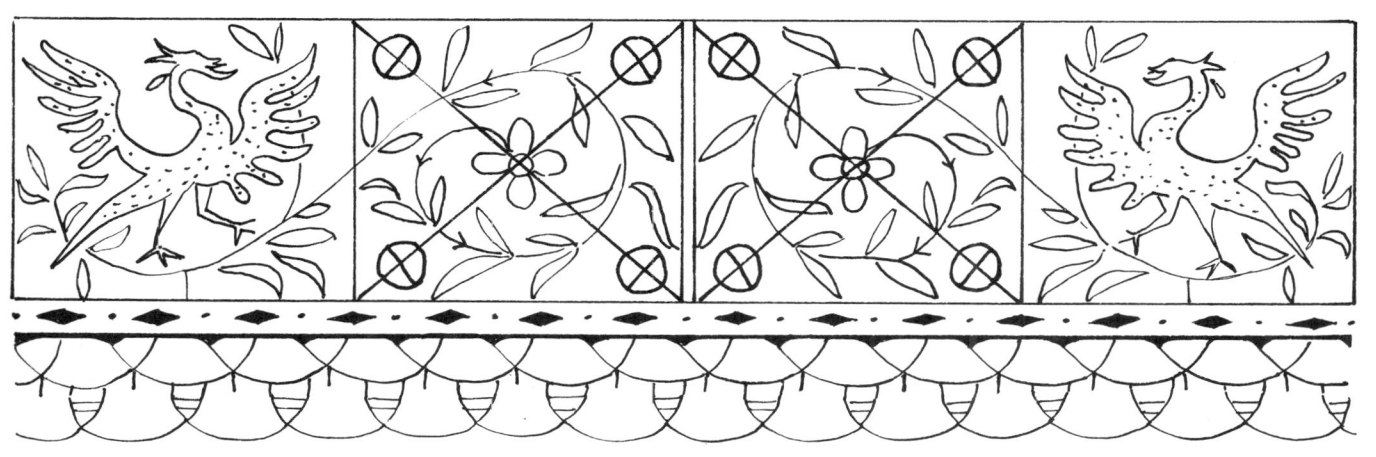

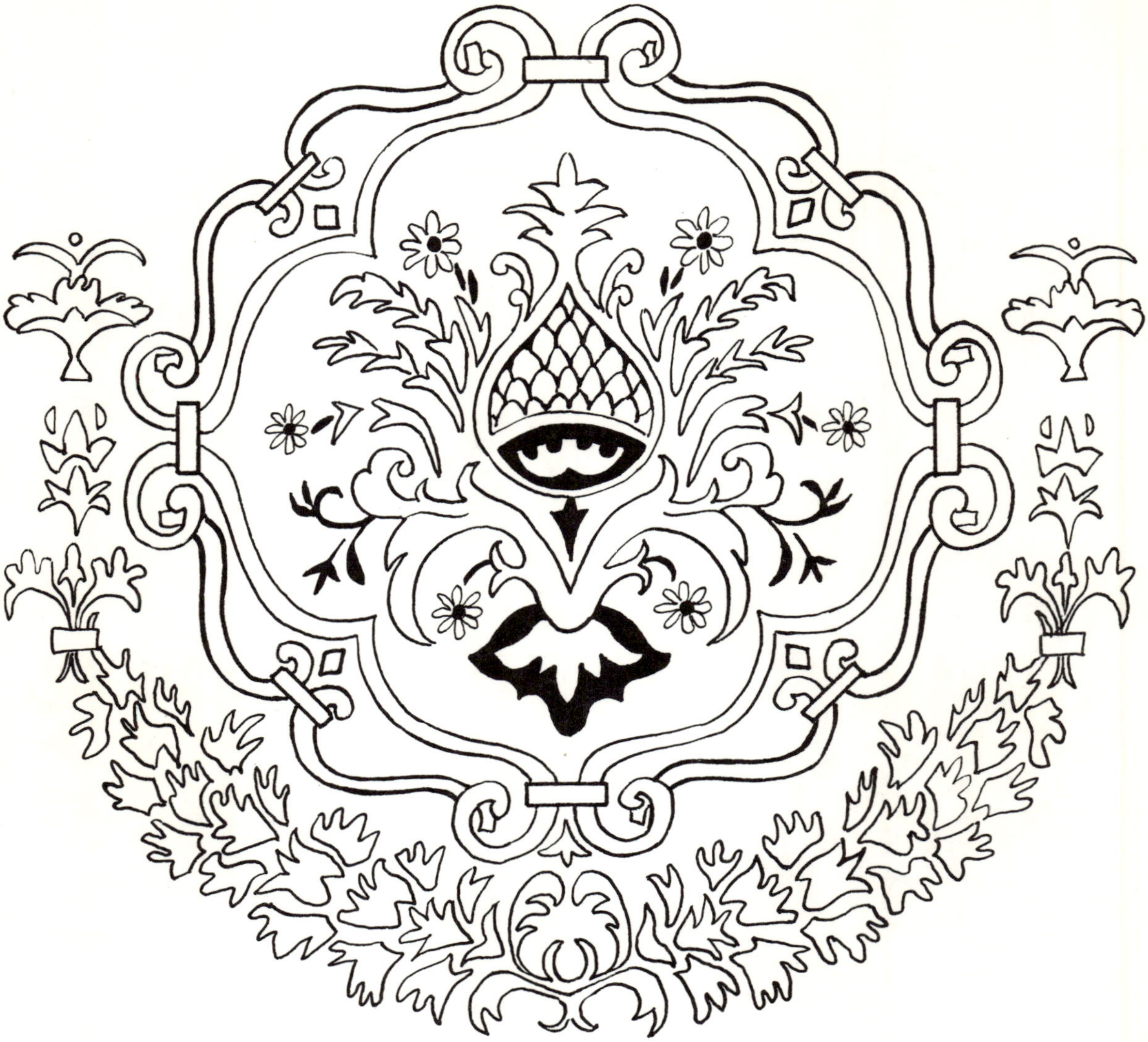

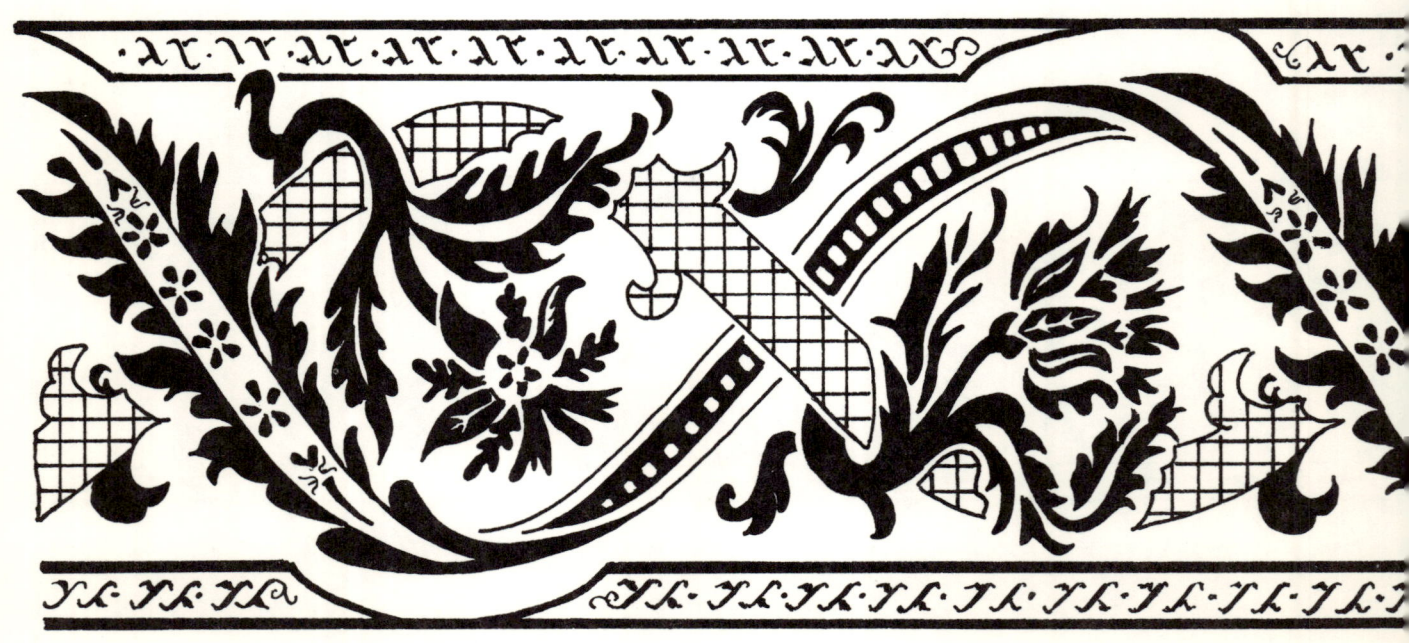

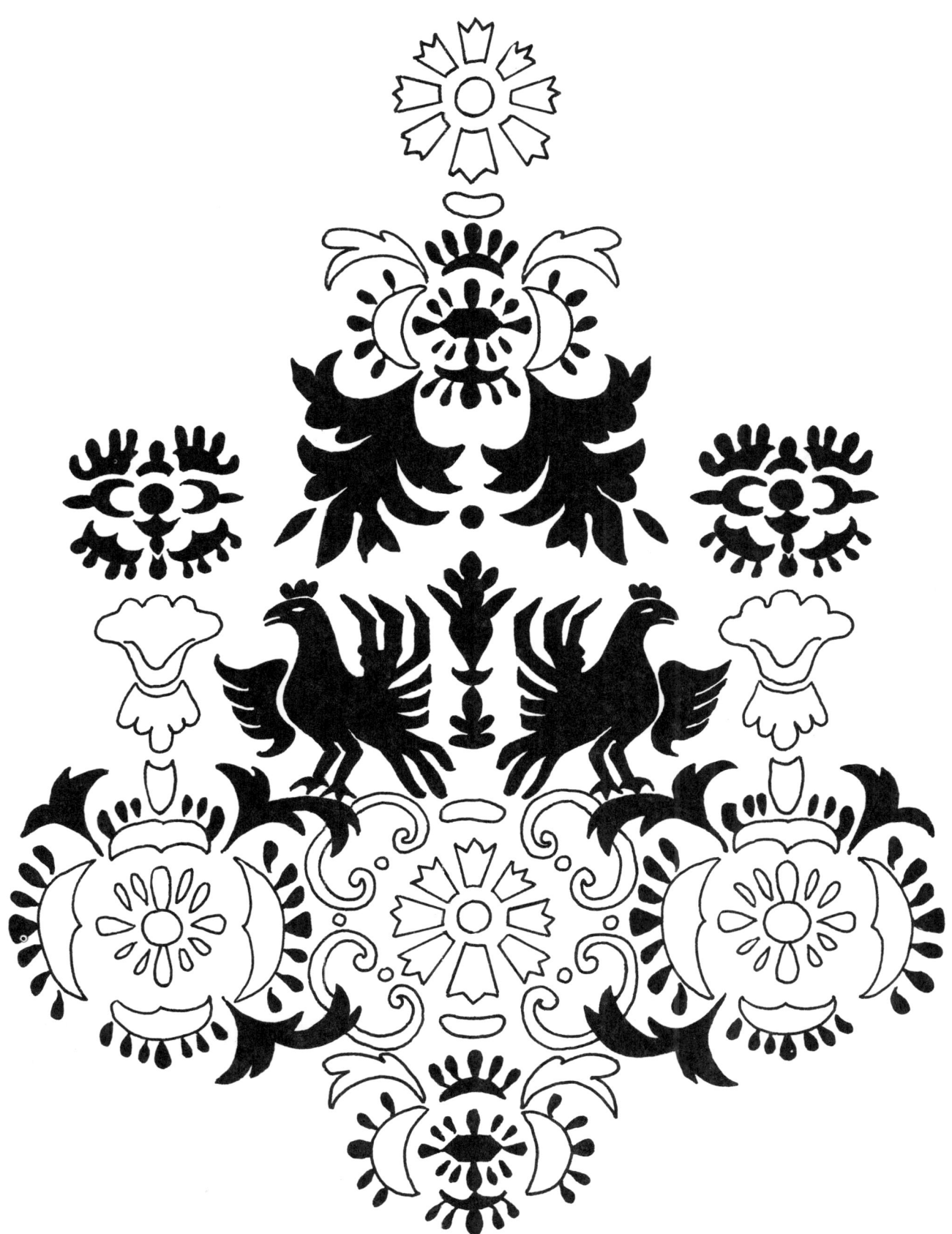

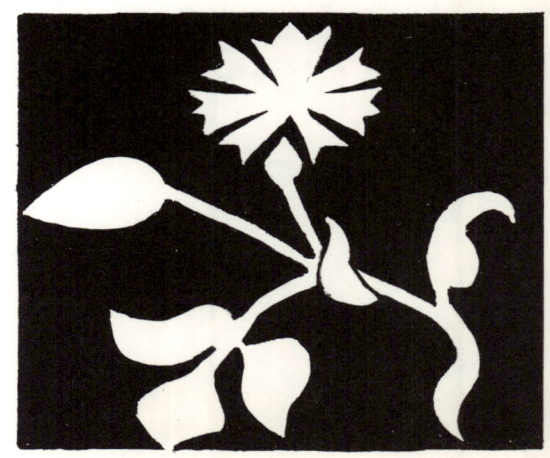

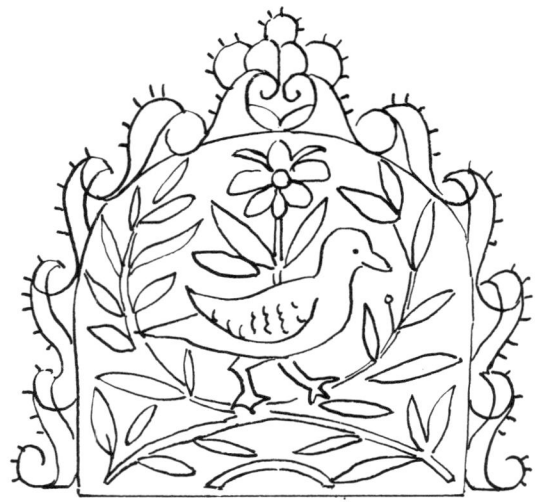

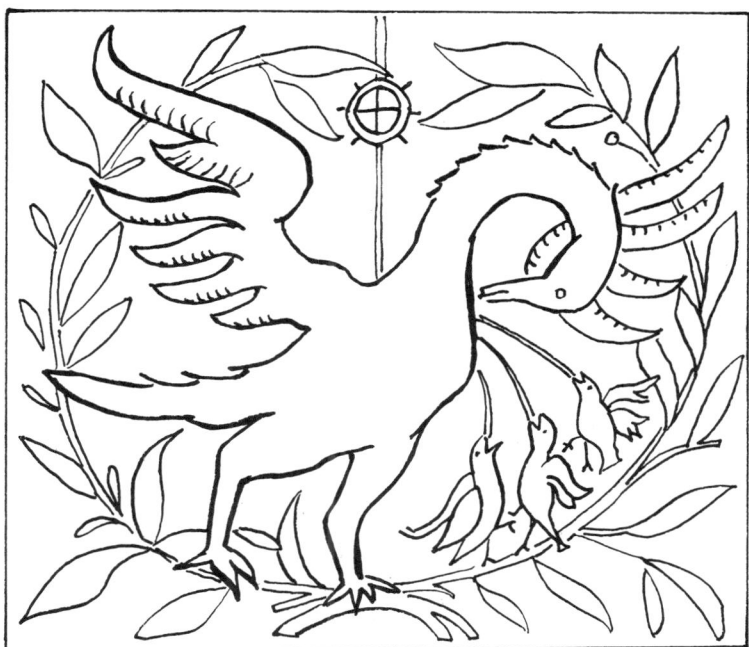
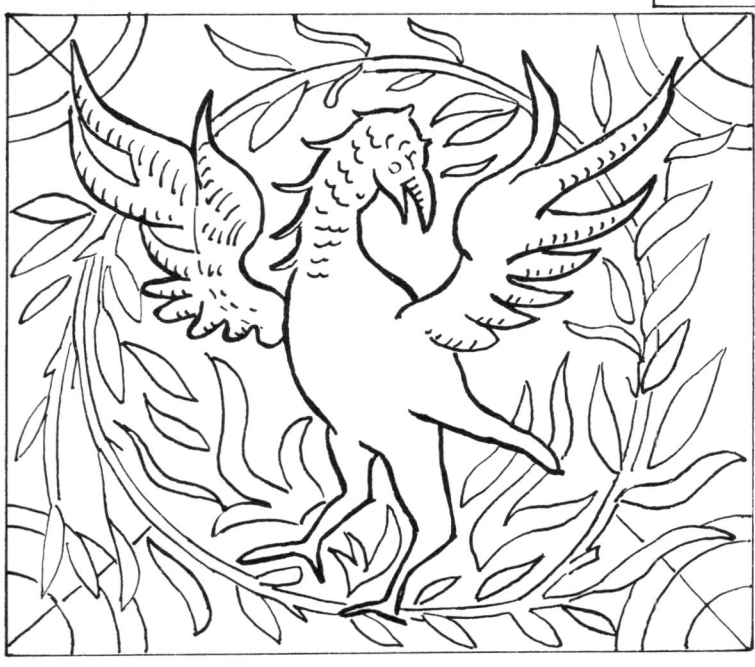

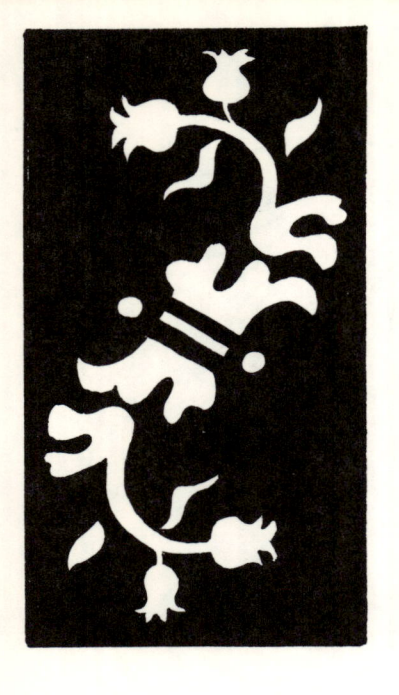
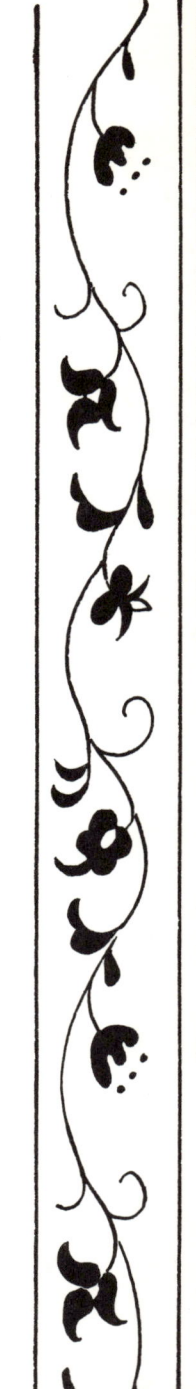
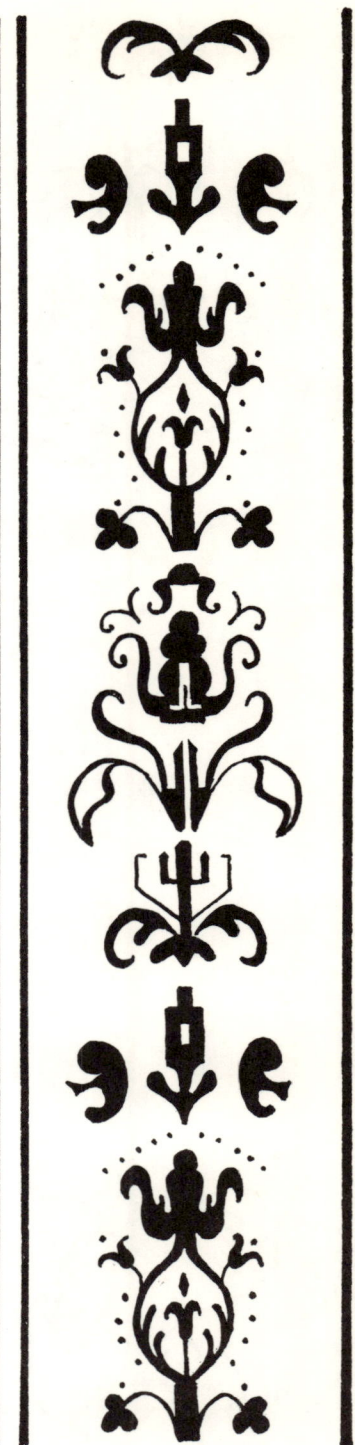

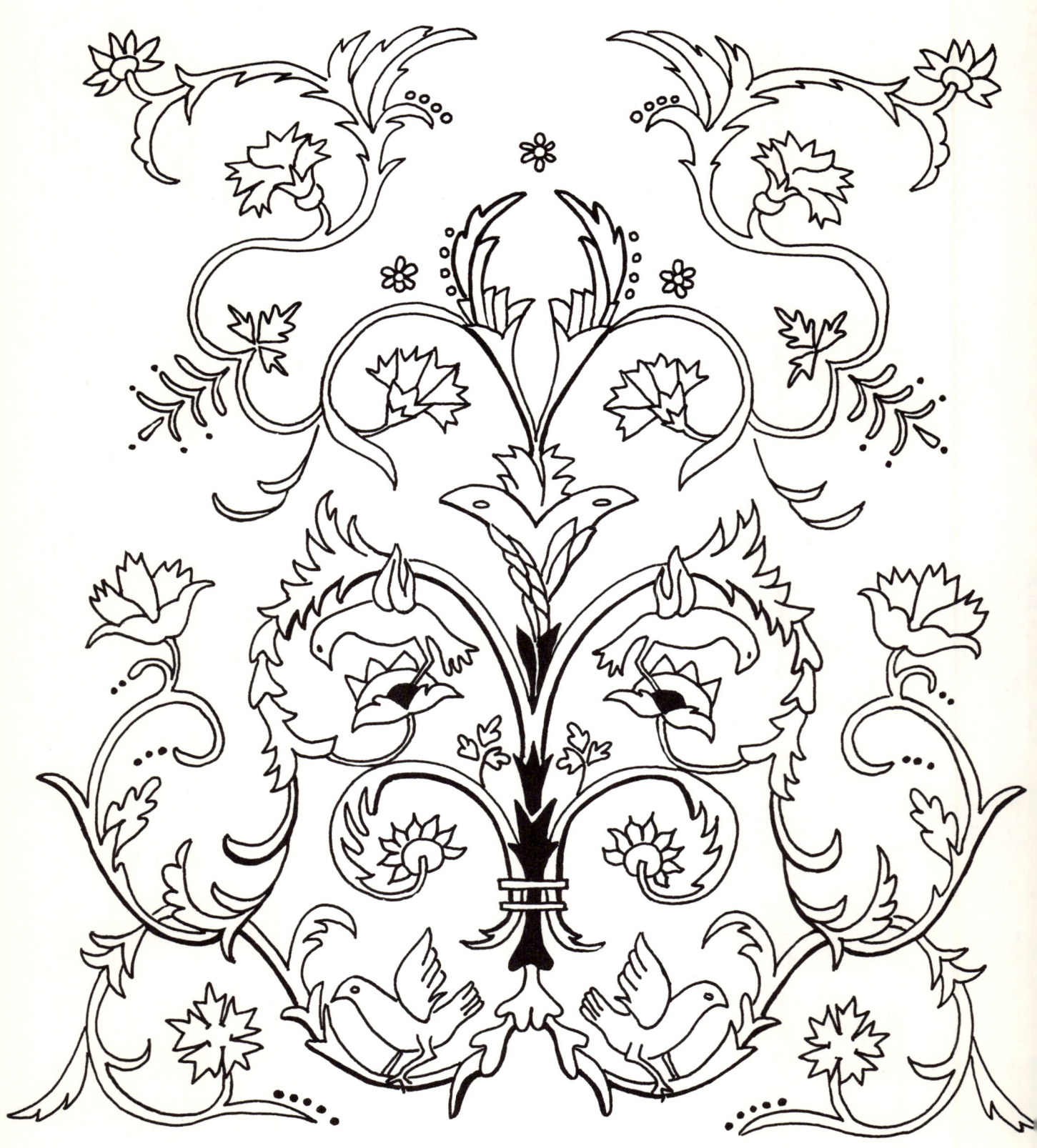

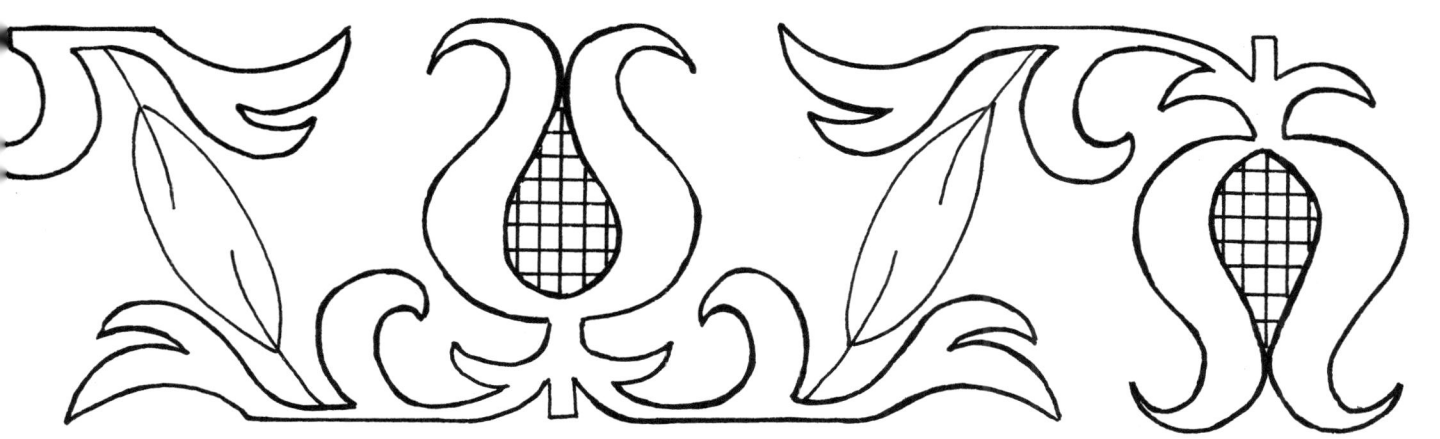

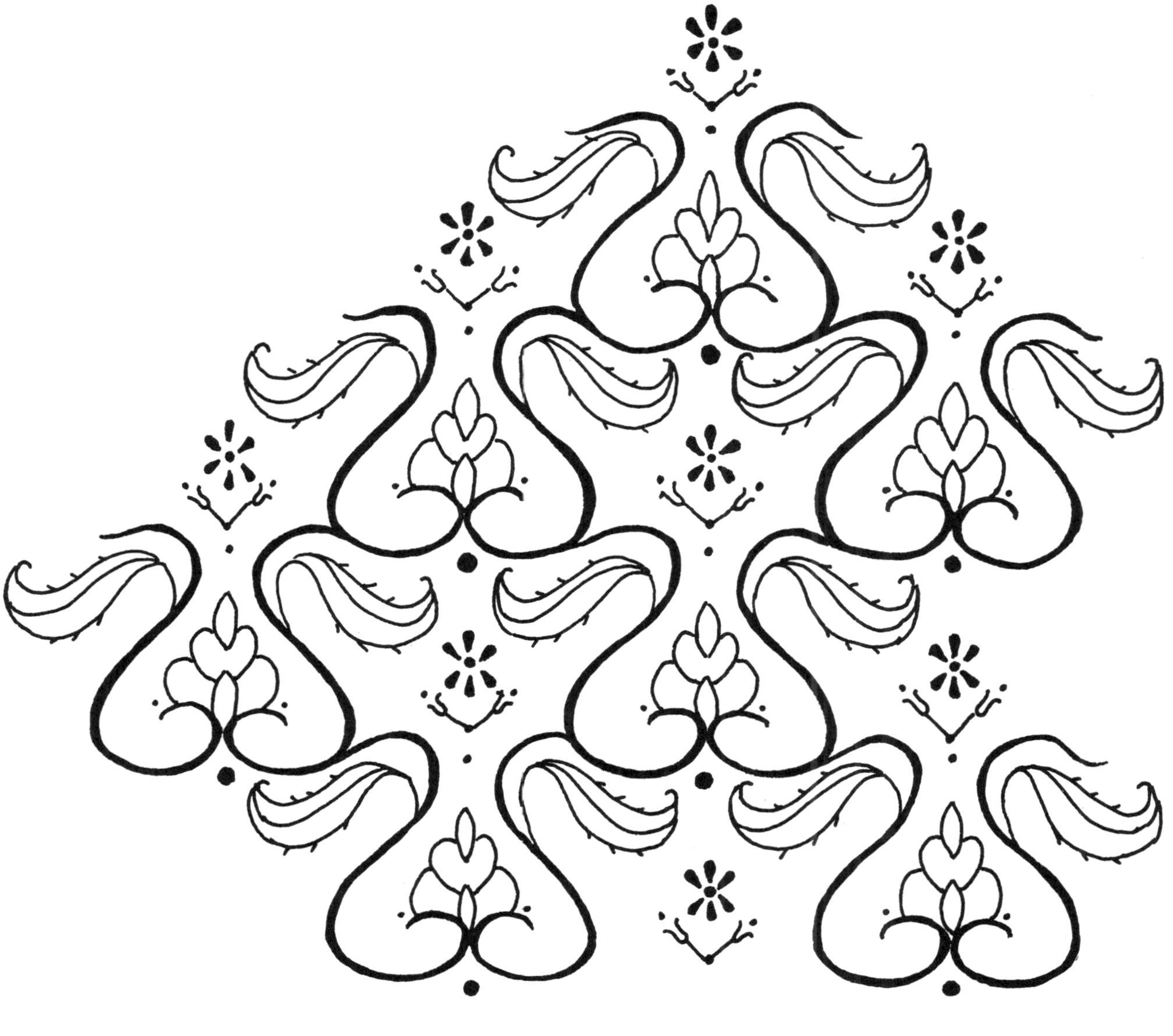

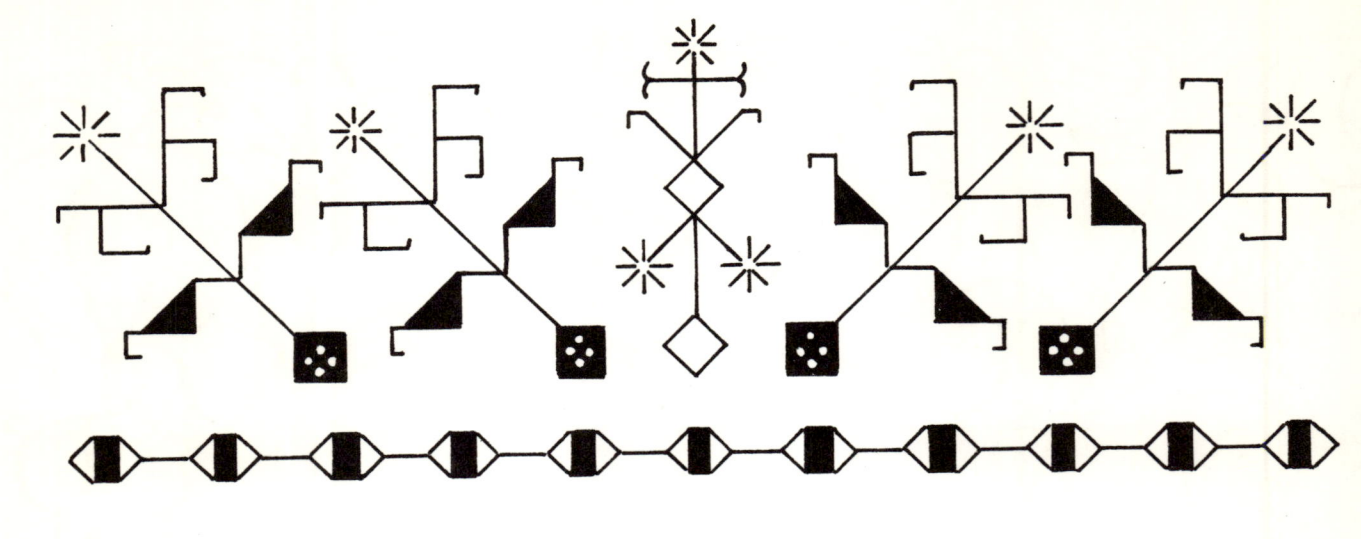

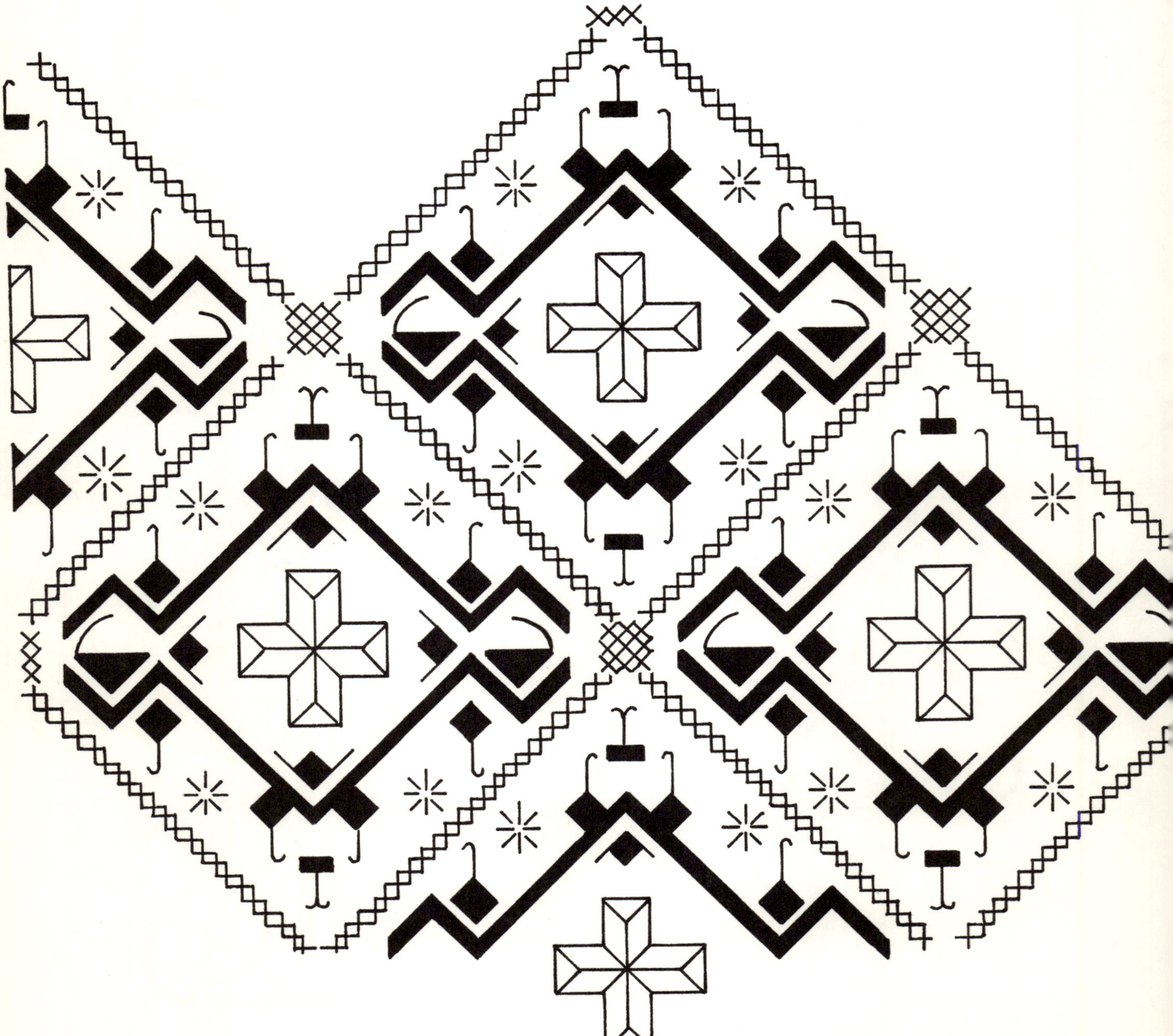

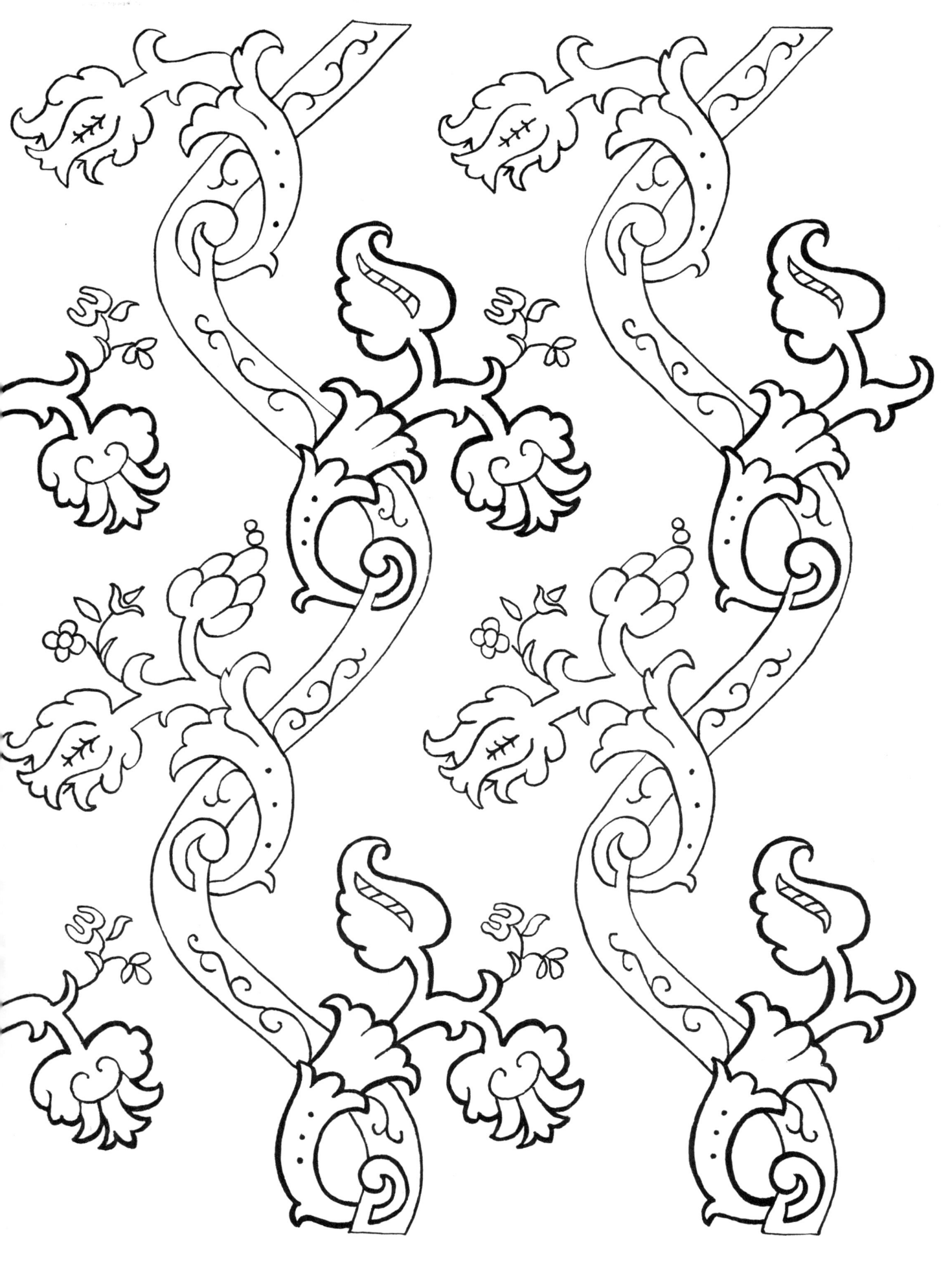

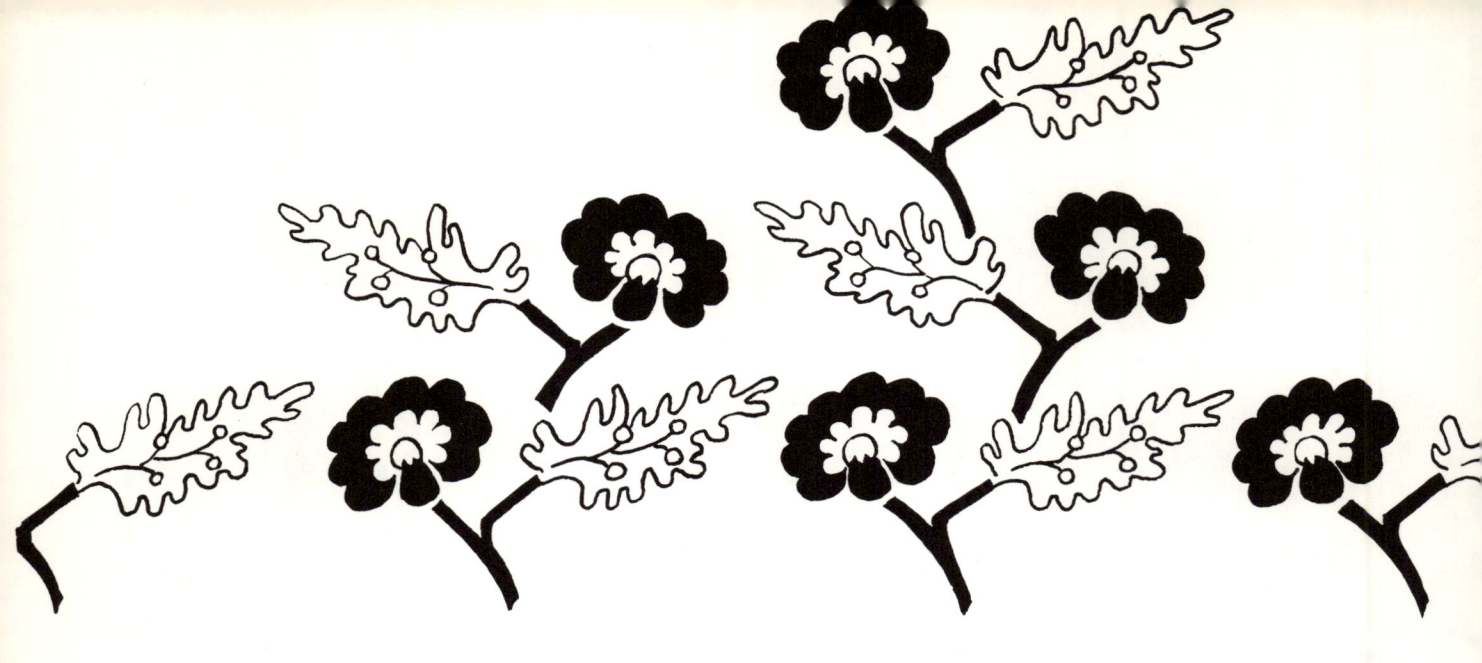

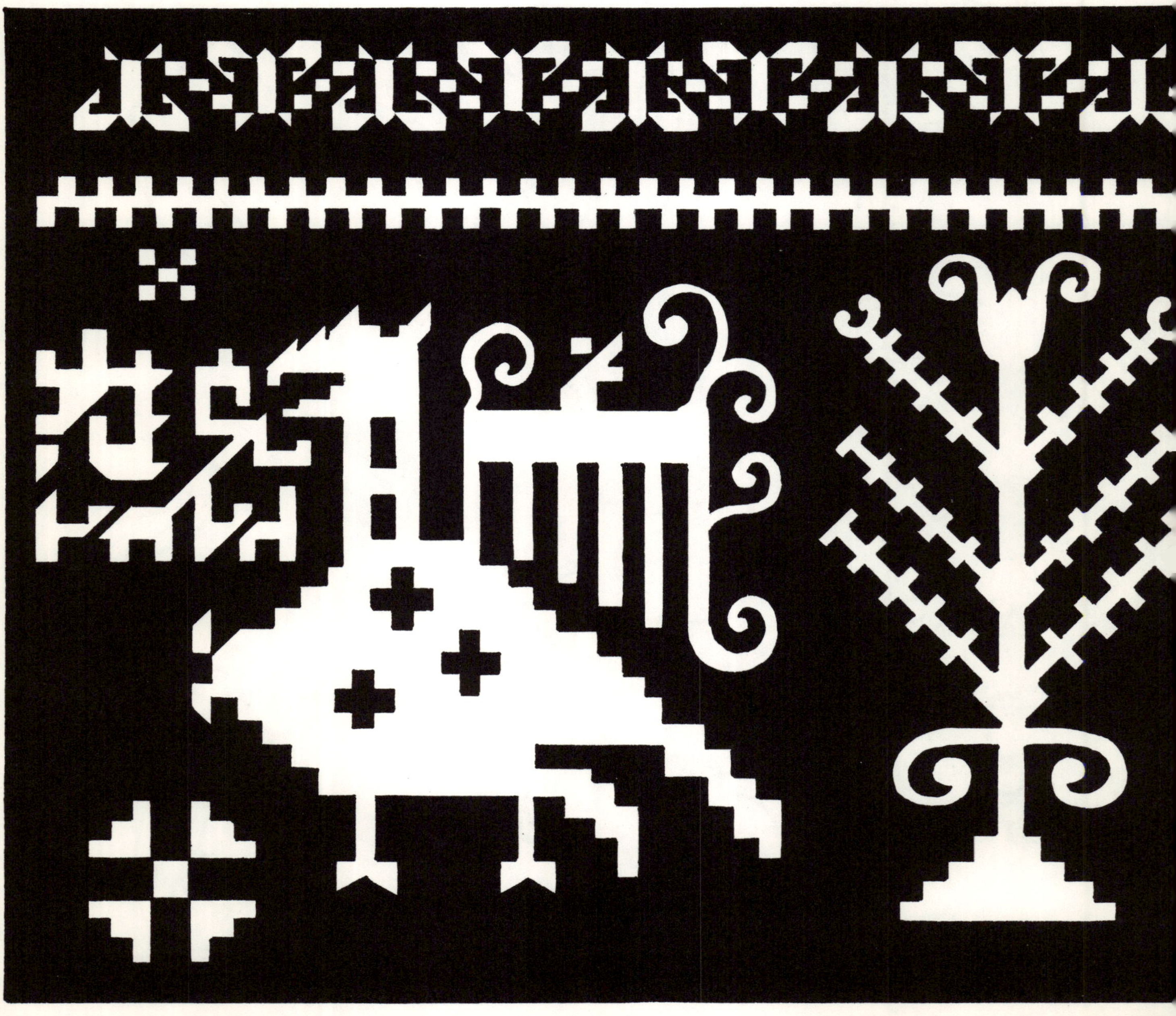

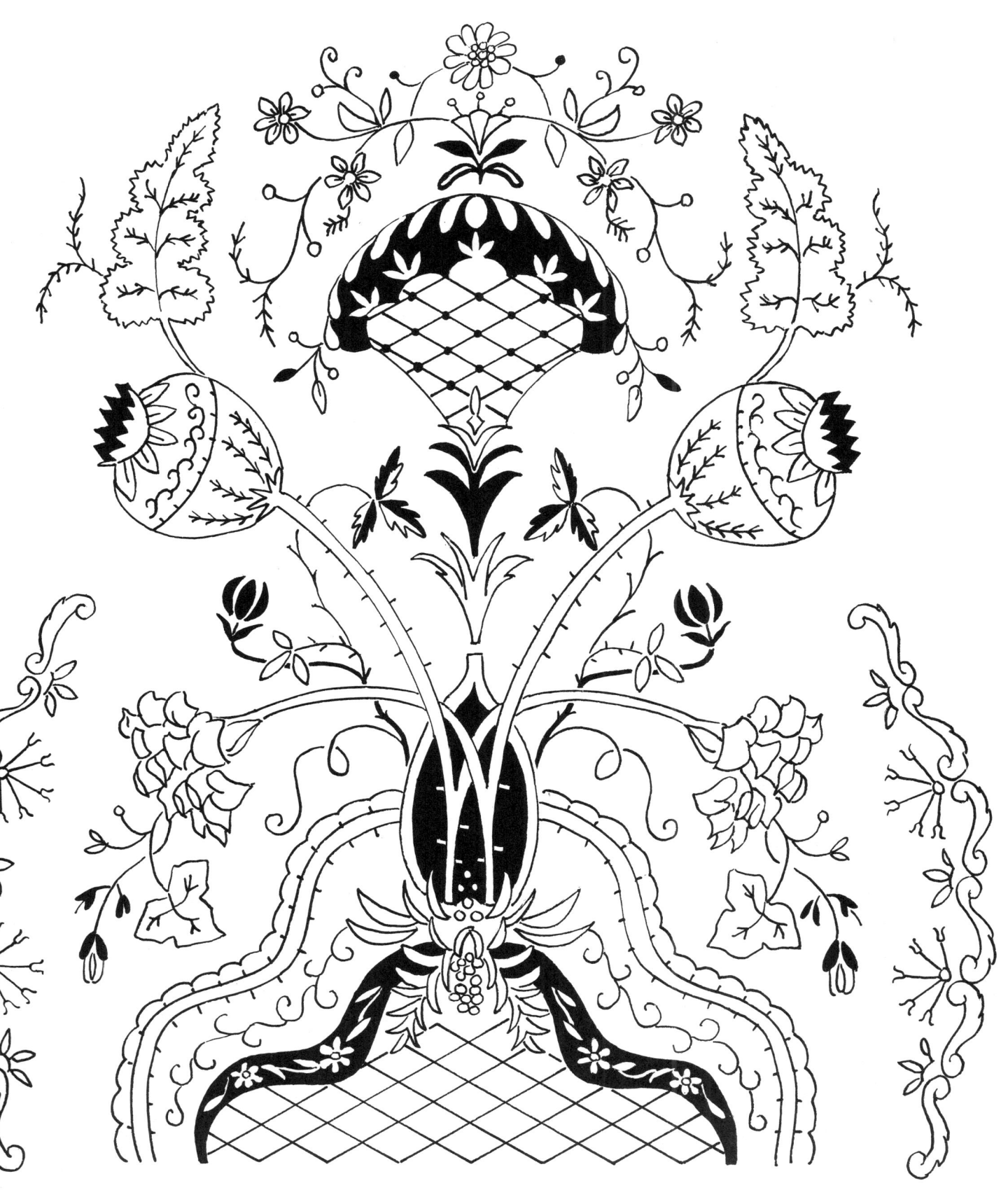

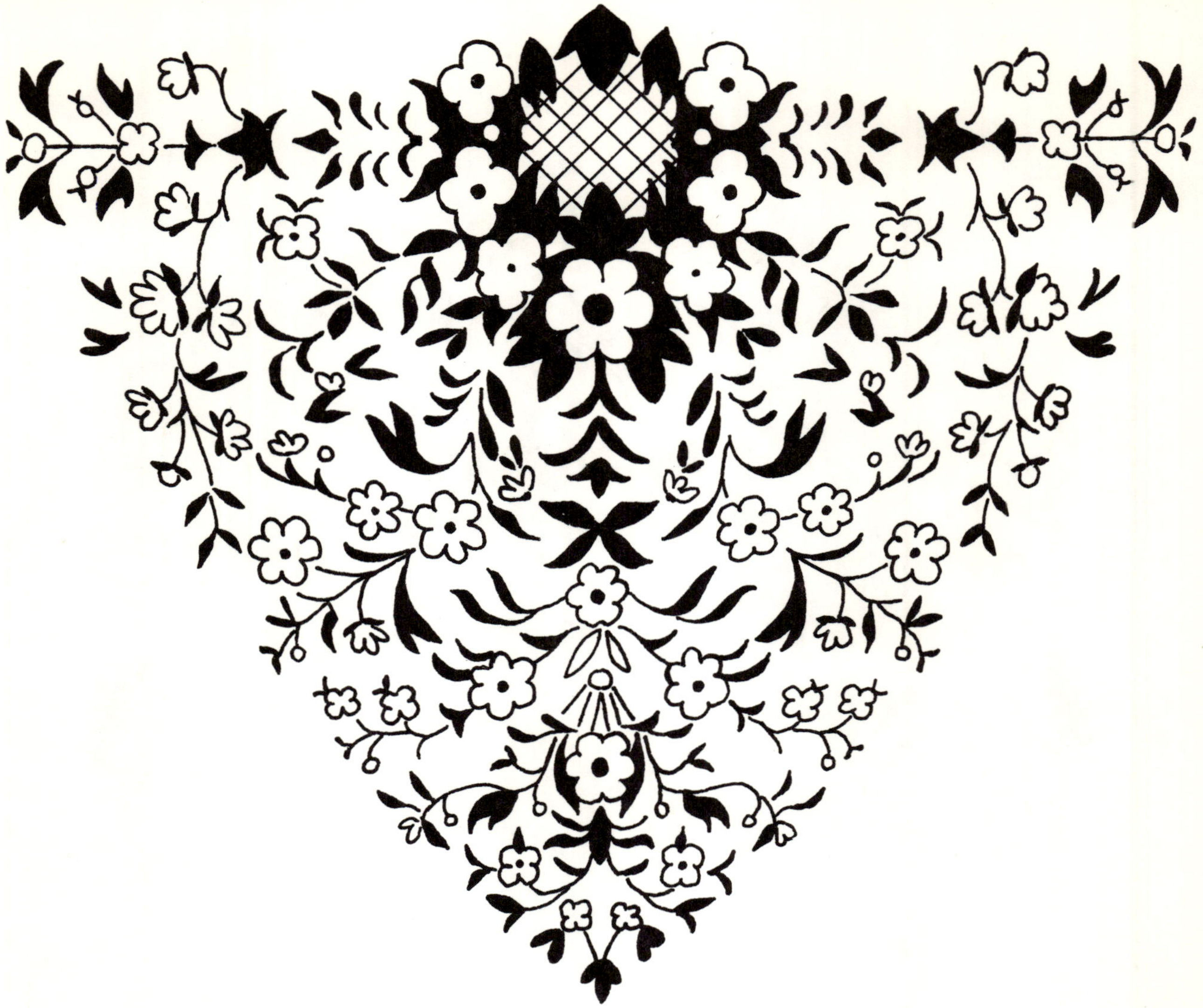

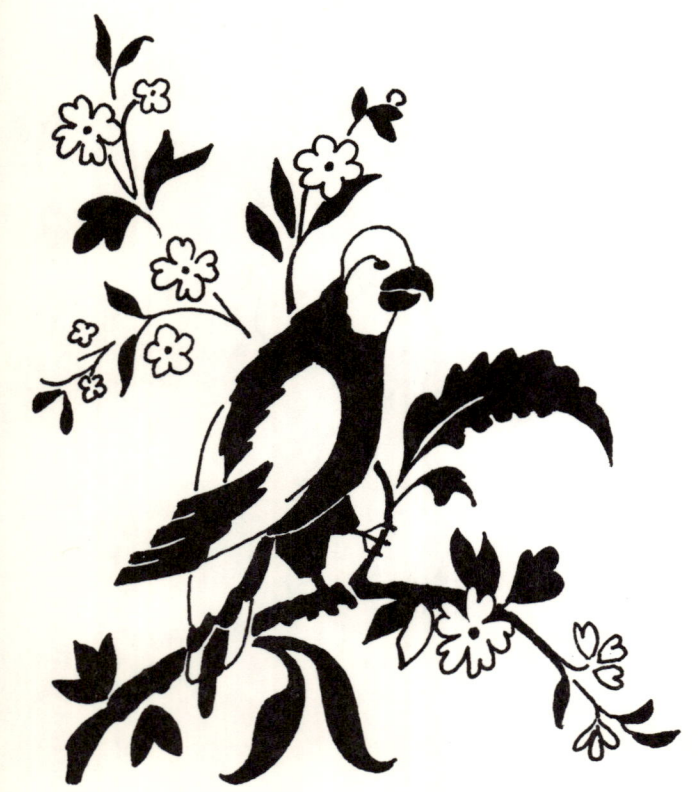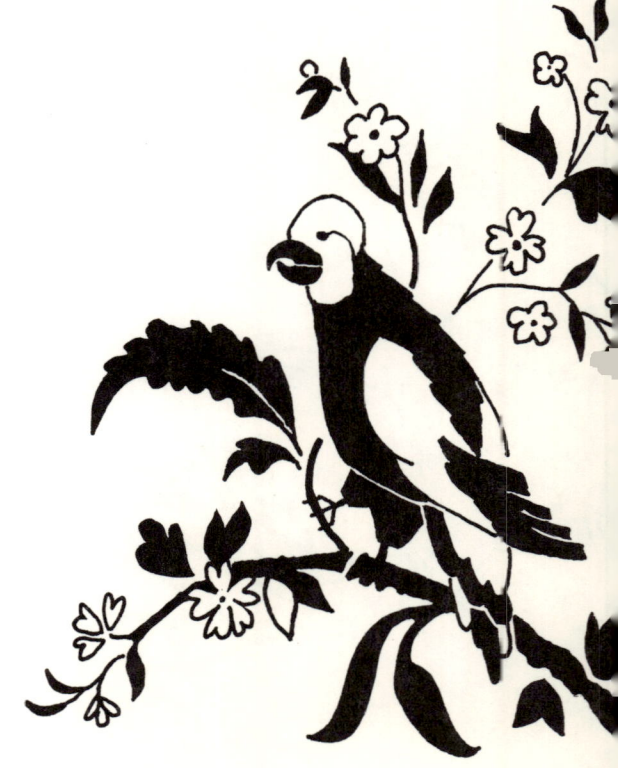

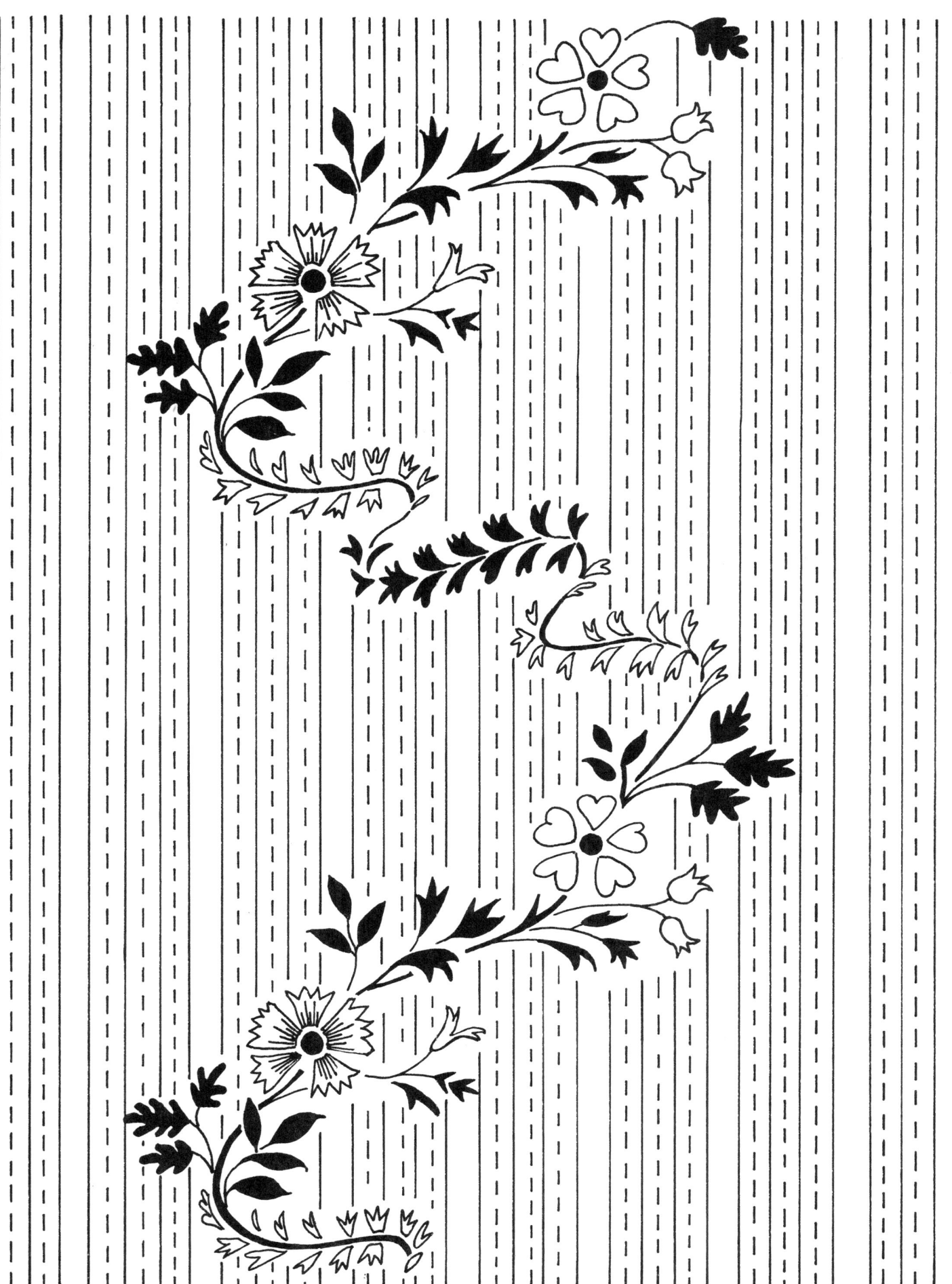

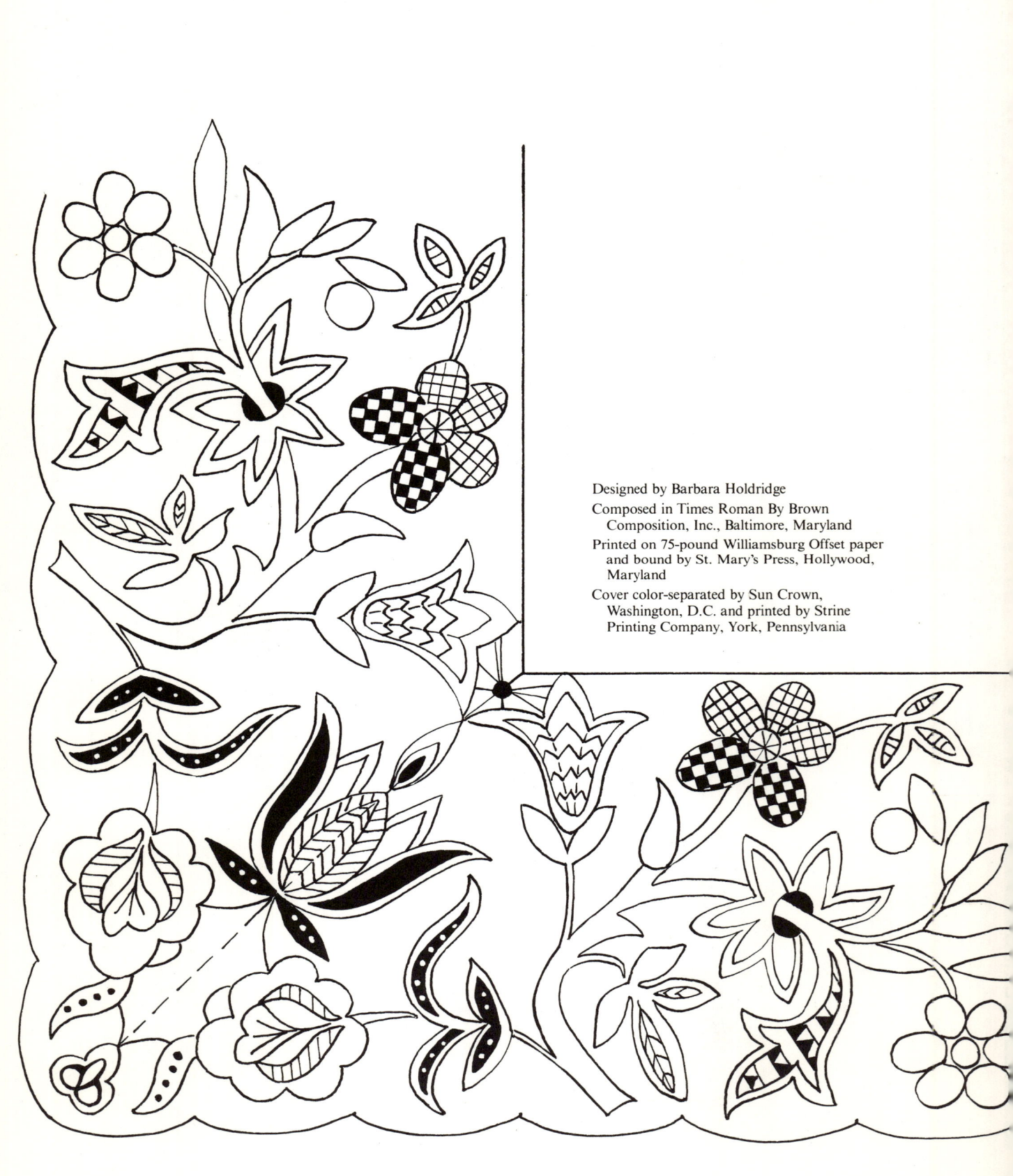

Designed by Barbara Holdridge

Composed in Times Roman By Brown Composition, Inc., Baltimore, Maryland

Printed on 75-pound Williamsburg Offset paper and bound by St. Mary's Press, Hollywood, Maryland

Cover color-separated by Sun Crown, Washington, D.C. and printed by Strine Printing Company, York, Pennsylvania